David Campbell:
writer, poet, storyteller, cultural ambassador.

David's boyhood in the ballad-rich northeast of Scotland gave him a lifelong love of poetry, story and song. This love infused his subsequent careers as teacher/radio producer/writer and storyteller.

Always a leader, as a youngster he had a gang with a homemade broadcasting service, Olympic games, plays and Tomsawyerish adventures.

David organised Fort Knox, the very first highly acclaimed Edinburgh Festival Fringe multi-complex. This featured the foremost Scottish poets, a fashion show, two plays in repertoire, one co-written by David, two late-night revues, five art exhibitions and a café.

In BBC Scotland he contributed imaginative educational and cultural programmes on Scottish writers and folklore. His ground-breaking radio drama series, *Kilbreck*, highlighted the cultural life and health concerns of the Scottish nation. The series gained a cult following.

He has published poetry, children's books, a book on Celtic story and lore, a significant two volume biography of the iconic Scottish traveller Duncan Williamson – *A Traveller in Two Worlds* – and most recently his memoir, *Minstrel Heart*, with Luath Press.

David is a cultural catalyst, and worldwide ambassador of Scottish heritage, literature and story.

By the same author:

Tales to Tell I, Saint Andrew Press, 1986
Tales to Tell II, Saint Andrew Press, 1994
The Three Donalds, Scottish Children's Press, 1996
Out of the Mouth of the Morning, Luath Press, 2009
A Traveller in Two Worlds Vol I, Luath Press, 2011
A Traveller in Two Worlds Vol II, Luath Press, 2012
Minstrel Heart: A Life in Story, Luath Press, 2021
Poems 1960–2020, Main Point Books, 2023

Story Harvest

DAVID CAMPBELL

ORKNEYOLOGY
PRESS

Published by Orkneyology Press
Stromness, Orkney Islands

ISBNs:
978-1-915075-03-1 – hardback
978-1-915075-04-8 – paperback
978-1-915075-05-5 – ebook

www.orkneyology.com
Book Sales:
https://shop.orkneyology.com/collections/orkneyology-press-books

All rights reserved. The contents of this book may not be reproduced in any form without written permission from the publishers, except for short extracts for quotation or review.

Typeset by
Main Point Books, Edinburgh

Text © David Campbell 2023
Cover image © Astrid Jaekel 2023

For Duncan Williamson

Contents

Preface by Donald Smith	9
Story Harvest	11
Lady of Many Colours	13
The Man Who Had No Story to Tell	16
Eric Liddell	20
Loch Lomond	26
Loch Lomond (song)	32
The Rout of Moy	33
MacCrimmon's Lament (song)	36
Seventeen Coffins	37
The Twice-Hanged Man	40
The Harper's Pass	43
The Blind Piper	47
The Coo That Ate the Piper	61
The Trowie Wedding	67
Jimmy Allen	74
Savourna	80
Off to Kintail	87
Yuki-Onna	93
Gregor Armstrong	102
The Minister and the Skull	110
The Holy Horse	116
Archie's Besom	121
Auld Cruvie	125
The Well of Youth	131

The Makers of Dreams	136
The Firetail	140
Caolte the Swift	146
The Sweetest Music	148
The Young Hero's Children	150
Arthur and the Hag	159
Oi and Yalasid	164
The Lonely Fisherman	169
Selchie of Sule Skerrie	178
The Sound of the Surge of the Sea	197
An Ataireachd Ard	202
The Iron Cold Winter	203
Jack and the Silver Shilling	208
Queen With the Cold, Cold Heart	214
The Little Squirrel	220
Star Apple	225
Archie Beag	228
Erchie Campbell	234
The Water of Life	238
Hiro the Gambler	241
The Poor Farmer	247
The Tax Collector at Jericho	249
Christmas Bell	256
The Caged Bird	260
Fat Murray	263
Goodbye	266
The Flying Horse of Earthdom	272
Acknowledgements	285

Preface

No-one has done more for the art of storytelling than David Campbell.

For David, stories well told are spoken poetry, and he has devoted decades to doing just that, supremely well.

However, the art of storytelling is much more than technique. Telling a story, according to Duncan Williamson, David's bosom friend and fellow storyteller, is passing on a gift to cherish. David Campbell's concern has always been to render that gift unique, generous and precious.

This gifting is part and parcel of David's wider generosity of spirit. For him love and friendship are not quantities to be allocated but qualities to be multiplied in the sharing. That is why, despite appearances in numerous festivals at home and abroad, storytelling ceilidh has always been the hearth of David Campbell's art – with all comers welcomed and affirmed. The Harvest gathered in this book is rich in stories heard and shared.

Moreover, David's own Edinburgh home has been an unfailing heart of hospitality and storytelling hand-in-hand. There should be an everlasting plaque at the stair entry: HERE BE STORIES – ENTER WITHIN.

It was Stanley Robertson, another with Duncan Williamson of the Scottish Traveller Tradition bearers, who used to say 'a story should be told eye to eye, mind to mind and heart to heart'. That points to a deeper inward dimension of storytelling. Within David's genial persona is a loyal friend, a listening ear, and a readiness to support people through rough times. He espouses the steadfast human values of compassion, respect and dignity; and acts on them quietly.

Around that core humanity, and sometimes personal struggles, David weaves a tapestry of fun and humour – a force field of grace and wit – by which he is often remembered. A phone call from David always includes at least one joke, usually unrepeatable. He sometimes threatens a collected edition of his jokes, but publishers beware!

On a few occasions David has experienced knockback against his elf of mischief, but no harm is ever intended, and he is the first to laugh at a joke against himself. On one occasion he severely instructed a packed house at the Scottish Storytelling Centre to switch off all mobile phones before he would begin. Ten minutes later, in a full on dramatic pause, a mobile went off on full volume. David glared, audience members looked round anxiously, till it became apparent that the call tone was coming from David's own sporran…

David Campbell has always been ready to share his repertoire of stories with others, eye to eye, and in print. This *Story Harvest* contains some of his favourite and most performed tales. It is beautifully produced by people who love and understand storytelling. Please read, tell and enjoy.

Thank you, David, from your wide community of friends, and from all the new friends this book will gain. Let the ceremony of delight continue. This is a harvest that never stops giving, and never wears out.

Donald Smith
Director, Scottish International Storytelling Festival
July 2023

Story Harvest

Since childhood I have reaped the benefit of many crops of stories from different fields; from my family, my reading, fortuitous meetings and, in the last forty years, from my worldwide travels and immersion in the pantheon of Scottish and Celtic folktales, particularly enriched by my twenty-year friendship with the master, tinker-Traveller Duncan Williamson.

Duncan's repertoire runs into hundreds of stories, songs and ballads he had avidly collected over his lifetime. These he shared with his philosophy, which I espouse, that a story is a gift to be passed freely on.

The stories in this selection reflect the generosity I have met in my worldwide storytelling travels, everything from jokes to epic tales, from Alaska to New Zealand. My criteria for telling any story, is that I've fallen in love with it and, like Duncan, see it as a gift to pass on. As he would say in this riddle:

> *This thing will never break,*
> *it will never wear out,*
> *you can give it away and still have it,*
> *if you don't give it away it is of no use.*

I love stories because, as the wonderful Traveller Stanley Robertson would say, 'They speak eye to eye, mind to mind and heart to heart.' My conviction is that in a world in which technology separates as well as connects people, being face to face with a live audience makes the deepest connection. As the novelist EM Forster said, 'Only connect.' Stories do that.

Lady of Many Colours

This is my memory of a tale I heard in Tel Aviv when I was on a storytelling trip with Duncan Williamson and Michael Kerins. I've told it my way, now you tell it your way.

Nobody noticed her, the little ragged girl,
    like a little gypsy girl,
    a barefoot gypsy in fluttering rags
running about the market place,
    running here, there and everywhere,
    a bright shadow
        looking for a place to rest,
        a place to stay.

And nobody seemed to see her:
    the merchants were so busy
        buying, selling, bartering, bargaining,
        making money, making deals.
    They didn't see her.
    Too busy, too busy,
        cutting corners, getting rich.
        They didn't see the little ragged girl.

And in the shadows sat the gamblers
    lurking, waiting, watching
        for the get-rich-quickers,

>   tricksters chasing shekels,
>   taking no chances in their games of chance,
>   winking, hoodwinking.
> The gamblers had no eyes to see her beckoning,
>   the little ragged girl.

And in their halls the lawyers walked and stalked,
       grave and grey and greedy,
       sombre and serious
       and gowned in mystique,
prowling the labyrinths of law,
       and costing a fortune.
They did not see her plight
       nor hear the plea
             of the little ragged girl.

And in their tents and stalls
       fortune-tellers gazed in crystal,
             talking stars.
They missed the light of hope
       dancing in her gypsy eye.

Lovers full of dreams,
       promising the sun and moon and stars,
       did not see her fluttering by.

Nor all the rascals and rogues,
       and cheats and vagabonds,
       seducers, tricksters of the human heart.

None saw the girl in rags
       who flitted through the marketplace.

But everyone saw the glittering lady
       gowned in colours of the earth and sea and sky

who laughed and sang and sighed
    as she went gliding by.

Everyone followed her.
    She, so full of surprises,
    light and dark and mystery.

Wherever she stopped, crowds gathered
    and listened, listened,
    listened to the colours in her words,
    flowing or tumbling, bright or dark or still.
    Everyone gathered to listen,
        saint and tinker,
        rich and poor and beggar and thief.

'Who is she?' thought the little, ragged wanderer,
    and, as dark fell, shyly she came to her
    and asked, 'Who are you? And why
    does everybody come and listen?'

'Why,' said the glistening woman, 'I am STORY
and that is why everybody wants me. And who are you,
little, ragged girl that no one seems to see?'

'Why,' said the girl, 'I am TRUTH. Will you take
me with you?'

'Under my cloak, next to my heart,' said Story,
and together they have travelled ever since.

The Man Who Had No Story to Tell

The wonderful old Travelling man Willie McPhee was a fine piper, tinsmith, basket maker, singer and storyteller. He was staying with me at my flat one night with his wife Bella. Bella's face was lined and brown like a beautiful autumn leaf. Together they played the Jew's harp as a prelude to this tale. Following Willie's practice, I also tell it in the first person.

It was harvest time and, aged eighteen, I got a holiday job working on a farm on the west coast. The banter in the bunkhouse at night was an education, little of which my mother would have approved.

The work stacking sheaves of corn was finished, and the harvest being complete, the farmer held a ceilidh that evening in the barn.

I sat in a corner enjoying the ballad singing, storytelling, the fiddle playing, the penny whistle and bagpiping, all lubricated by drams of whisky. This was my first experience of whisky and such a ceilidh so I was feeling merry and delighted until the farmer turned to me and said, 'Well, Davey lad, it's time you gave us a tune.'

'I'm sorry,' I said, 'but I don't play anything and I don't sing.'

'What about a wee poem or a story then?'

'I don't know any poem or story to tell,' I said, feeling embarrassed to be the odd man out.

'Ach well,' said the farmer. 'You can do a wee forfeit. Go

down to the shore and bail the water out of the boat and that will do. Ye'll find the bailer in the boatie. Bring it back here when you've finished.'

'At least this is something I can do,' I thought. It was dark outside and the farmer gave me a lantern to see my way.

So I buttoned up my jerkin and set off. It was about a hundred yards to the shore and there at the water's edge was the boat. I left the lamp on the sand and as I climbed into the boat to get the bailer I slipped and fell and cracked my head.

When I came to, the full moon was shining bright and the boat was tilting and rocking. I was adrift and couldn't even see the lantern on the shore.

I got the oars and was rowing as hard as I could, but no sign of the lantern on the shore. The sea was choppy and the waves rising. I was a big strong lad at the time but I felt weak and could hardly pull on the oars.

'I'll need to have a smoke of my pipe,' I thought. My pipe was one of my ideas of 'being one of the men folk.'

I pulled the oars in and reached to my jerkin pocket to get my pipe and I felt a big lump. 'What's this?' I thought, and felt the other side. Another big lump! 'What's this?' I thought, 'Two big lumps.' Then I felt again. Instead of my jerkin something like a blouse of soft silk. 'Was this the whisky?' I thought. I put my hand up to scratch my head and felt beautiful, soft, long hair. On my legs, no trousers. A skirt! And I felt: something was gone! Something else in its place. I felt numb. Didn't know what to think. The waves were rising, getting higher. I tried to grab the oars but I was too weak to row. I fell back in the boat and lay there sobbing and greeting like a girl!

I fell asleep and when I wakened the sun was shining. The boat wasn't moving. It was beached but nowhere I recognised. 'What's going to happen to me?' I thought. 'I'm lost. And what's happened to me?'

The first thing I saw was a young man walking along the

beach. He came up to the little boat and said, 'Where did you come from, lassie?'

I didn't know what to say. 'I was shipwrecked I think. I don't know where I came from. I don't know what happened to me.'

'Well, you'd better come home with me and get some dry clothes. Some of your people I'm sure will be looking for you.'

So I went with him to a big house where he lived with his mother. She gave me some dry clothes, a skirt and blouse, and we sat down to a fine supper brought by a cook.

So there I stayed. I got used to being a woman and we fell in love, this young man and me. I said my name was Davina. He called me Divine Davina. In time we had a little boy and a little girl. Time passed and when the boy was ten and the girl seven, I went for a walk down by the shore. It was a lovely summer day. And there was a boat at the water's edge.

'I wonder,' I thought, 'is that the bailer that caused all this still there?'

I stepped into the boat. At that moment there was a flash of lightning, a crash of thunder and rain. I slipped and fell and I was out like a light.

When I came to, I was looking up at a cloudless starry sky. I saw the oars and began rowing weakly, but soon my arms felt stronger and I was pulling nice and strong with a good rhythm.

Then I noticed a funny farmyard smell off myself. It was the smell of sheep dip! I put my hands to my chest. Flat as a pancake. I was wearing my old jerkin, old trousers and coarse tackety boots. 'Oh,' I thought, 'this is terrible. Where is my husband, and my two children?' Then on the shore I saw a light and rowed hard and fast as I could to the shore. And there was the lantern still burning.

I beached the boat, pulled it well up and tied it to a rock and took the bailer with me. I saw the light from the barn and soon heard a ballad drifting through the dark. When I came into the barn it was just as I left it. The same farmhands. Everything the same.

'Well Davey, ye're back. Did you get the bailer?'

'There's your bailer,' I said, 'but you're never going to believe what happened to me!'

And I told the story start tae finish and everybody listened, completely silent.

'Well,' said the farmer, 'that's the best tall tale I've heard in a long while. And ye said ye had nae story! That's the best of the night!'

Eric Liddell

The great champion, Olympic athlete and legend, Eric Liddell, was my father's cousin. After this Christian hero, my younger brother was christened Eric Liddell Campbell. The story of this great man was part of our family lore. Perhaps it inspired the athletic aspirations and achievements of myself and my brother.

… for them that honour me I will honour, and they that despise me shall be lightly esteemed.
(1 Samuel 2:30b KJV)

Some people just seem to be remarkable, and this story tells of a remarkable Scotsman, remarkable in many ways, and about him many remarkable things were said. Some say he was Scotland's greatest athlete, some that he was the most popular and best-loved athlete Scotland ever produced. He was called 'the Scottish Superstar' of the 1920s and the film *Chariots of Fire* was about him. He was also called 'a traitor to his country.'

His name was Eric Henry Liddell and he became a legend in his lifetime. He was born not in Scotland, but in China, at the beginning of the twentieth century. His father was a Christian missionary and his mother a nurse, and they were delighted when she gave birth to a healthy little boy.

Little Eric, from the earliest times, loved to run, to take to the hills, bounding over them like a deer, his feet pounding to the rhythm of God in his heart.

But they that wait upon the Lord shall renew their strength;
They shall mount up with wings as eagles;
(Isaiah 40:31a KJV)

At school he proved to be a fine sprinter and, for a sprinter, had an unusual style. He would throw his head back and his arms would pump like pistons which is why he later came to be known as 'the Flying Scotsman' – after the fastest steam train of the age. By the time he went to university, his fame had spread.

At Edinburgh University he competed in the 100 yards, the 220 yards and the 440 yards races, today called the 100, 200 and 400 metres. Now the flower of Scotland's sprinters, he competed with competitors from England and abroad with resounding success. He became Scottish champion in the 100 and 220 yards races, equalled the Scottish record in the former and set a new record in the latter. He was capped as a Scottish Rugby internationalist where he, 'the Flying Scotsman,' played on the left wing. However, it was as an athlete that he was known far and wide.

Yet to Eric, more important than his beloved running, was his faith. At meetings all over the country, he spoke of the Christian God, one of his particular themes being the sanctity of the Lord's Day, Sunday: 'We should set one day apart for God. The Sabbath should be a day of gratitude for the gifts of all kinds that God has given us.' This rooted belief in the sanctity of the Sabbath was an unshakeable conviction.

In 1923 the Paris Olympic Games were a year away. That same year, at the Triple 'A' Championships in England, Eric won the 220 yards sprint and the 100 yards with a new British record that was to stand for fifty-five years.

A week later, Eric astonished experts in the world of sprinting. He was competing against the best international runners of England and Ireland in the taxing 440 yards sprint. As usual, before the race, he shook hands with all the runners. On their marks, first time they were off with the gun, sprinting from the line: Gillies, the English champion, and Liddell stride for stride when – a gasp from the crowd – Gillies bumped Liddell and the Scot crashed to the ground. When Eric raised his head, he was well behind the fastest men in Britain. For any normal person, that would have been the end of the race; not for the remarkable Eric. He sprang to his feet and gave chase, legs pounding, arms like pistons, the 'Flying Scotsman' at full steam. No one believed what they were seeing; it was impossible that he could catch up. But the glint had come into his eyes, his head lifted high as if his heart sang:

I will lift mine eyes unto the hills,
From whence cometh my help.
(Psalm 121:1 KJV)

His feet pounded, his chest pounded. He ran like a man inspired. He was gaining ground. The crowd was hushed; surely this was impossible. Then, as the runners burst into the home stretch, they saw Eric draw level with Gillies. They cheered; every voice was with him. He collapsed through the tape, first. Against all odds he had won.

Soon after this, Eric received a letter selecting him to run for Britain in the Paris Olympic Games, in the 100 metres. This was a high honour, to compete with the fastest men in the world in this most celebrated of Olympic events. He was overjoyed. Everyone in Scotland was proud, full of anticipation. Maybe one of their countrymen would be 'the fastest man on earth.'

Then the programme for the Olympic Games was announced. The heats for the 100 metres were to be on a Sunday.

Eric read the programme and simply said, 'I cannot run on a Sunday.' He sent a letter withdrawing from the Games.

People were aghast. 'You are mad to throw up this chance, the chance to be the fastest man on earth, to win an Olympic gold medal, to put Scotland on the map.'

'I keep Sunday aside for God,' he said.

'What about your country? You've been selected to represent Britain. You're no better than a traitor to your country!'

'I cannot be a traitor to God,' he said, and would not change his mind.

In dismay, the Olympic selection committee met. What were they to do? Their finest prospect would not run. At last someone said, 'Let Eric Liddell run the 400 metres. There are no Sunday heats for that race.' And so it was agreed that he would compete in the 400 metres, the longest, hardest and most punishing of the sprints.

It was 1924, a burning hot July day. Paris was crowded with people. The spectators were impatiently awaiting the final of the 400 metres. Even in the heat, the world record had been twice broken and the man who would not run on Sunday had got through to the Olympic finals!

But Eric drew the worst possible position – the dreaded outside lane where you could not see the other competitors. Inside him were the fastest runners in the world.

Suddenly, through the excited burbling of the crowd, the sound of the Scottish bagpipes filled the air. The finalists were waiting for the starter. Fitch, the American world record holder; Butler, the British record holder; Imbach, the Swiss champion; Taylor, another fast American, and on the outside, Eric Liddell.

The pipes died down. Eric Liddell shook hands with all the competitors. At that moment, a man ran up to him and gave him a little note with a message written on it. Eric read the paper and clasped it in his hand. The competitors were called to the starter's orders. The whole stadium grew hushed and silent.

The gun cracked! Eric flew from the start, arms flailing,

legs driving. Halfway, he was in the lead. The crowd was frantic. He surely couldn't keep this up. He drove on. The Englishman was gaining on him. Fitch, the world record holder, was closing the gap. At fifty metres to go, Eric flung back his head and sped on like a man looking to the hills, inspired by God ... *I will lift up mine eyes unto the hills, from whence cometh my aid* ... he drew ahead and, setting a new world record, Eric Liddell broke the tape to the wild cheering of the Olympic crowd.

It was the most popular win of those Olympic Games, probably of any Olympic Games ever.

Eric returned to face a hero's welcome in Edinburgh. As the train pulled into Waverley Station, he found the platform crowded with well-wishers. He was jostled, congratulated and cheered. A homecoming to remember for the man who refused to run on a Sunday.

At Eric's graduation ceremony from Edinburgh University, the normally sombre principal cracked a joke saying, 'Mr Liddell, none can pass you except the examiner!' The students crowned him with a laurel wreath and carried him shoulder high through the town to the kirk of St Giles.

In his honour the Lord Provost gave a dinner. Everyone had heard of his triumph and people were curious to know what was in the note he'd been handed before his famous victory.

'Getting that note is one of my finest memories,' said Eric. 'One of the trainers handed it to me. It came from my favourite book, the Bible, and said, "He that honours me, I shall honour."'

The audience rose to its feet in tribute to this modest man who put his God before fame or popularity, or even his country.

The athletics world lay at his feet.

'Where now? The sky's the limit,' said his friends. 'What will be your next race?'

'China,' said Eric.

'China?' they asked. 'China?!!!'

'Yes, China,' said Eric. For him, God's next race was of a different kind, as long and hard and as gruelling as the 400 metres, with no cheering crowds. Eric was going to do God's work as a missionary.

So he left the fame, the world of athletics and his native Scotland to work with the people of China. As with his running, he gave it everything he had, went full out from the start. This time the race of his life ran into the full horror of World War II.

Along with thousands of others, separated from his wife and family, Eric was imprisoned by the Japanese. Prison camp needed all his courage, all his stamina and all his faith in God. And that is what he gave: he worked endlessly and tirelessly, helping other prisoners, organising games for the young folk, comforting the sick and dying. In the end the effort killed him.

In 1945, shortly before the war ended, he collapsed and died. This remarkable man had run to the end of his life's race.

Loch Lomond

The spirit of loyalty of the followers of the Bonnie Prince is encapsulated in this song, 'The Bonnie Banks of Loch Lomond'. This heroic, but ill-fated, campaign, with its disastrous consequences is, as they say, the stuff of legend.

A tune recognized the world over,
    a chorus sung the world over:

> *Ye'll tak the high road and I'll tak the low road,*
>   *And I'll be in Scotland afore ye,*
>   *But me and my true love we'll never meet again*
>   *On the bonnie, bonnie banks of Loch Lomond.*

A bonnie tune
    about a bonnie place,
but a sad song that tells a sad story.

And the story begins not on the bonnie banks of Loch Lomond
    but in the sweet, green valley of
      Glenfinnan.

There, on the nineteenth of August in the year 1745,
  the bonnie prince,
    Bonnie Prince Charlie,
      Prince Charles Edward Stewart,

raised his standard to reclaim the British throne.

The clans rose from glen to glen
>	to the sound of the great pipes,
>		the war pipes,
>	to the fiery cross on the hill tops,
>		to the call of the prince.

Cameron of Lochiel,
>	the Stewarts of Appin,
>		Clan Ranald Macdonald,
>	a thousand clansmen swept southwards,
>		gathering numbers as they marched.

And near our bonnie, bonnie banks of Loch Lomond
>	in Glen Endrick
two Maclain clansmen were talking of the prince's cause:
Fergus, a seasoned warrior, and young Donald,
>	clansman and friend.

'Donald, will you follow the prince?'
'That I will Fergus, to the death.'
'And what of your lass, what of Mary?'
'Tonight when we will meet on the shores
of Loch Lomond, I will tell her.'

And that night,
>	in the shimmering, long half-light
>		of the gloaming,
when the afterglow of the sun purpled the highland hills,
>	they met on the steep, wooded side of Ben Lomond.

And as Donald approached,
>	Mary could see a cloud on his brow:
'Donald,' she said, 'what is the dark cloud on your brow?'

'It is the cloud that keeps the prince
    from his rightful place on the throne, Mary,' he said.
'I am going to follow the prince.'

'I'll wait for you, Donald,' she said.
            'I'll be here.'
But a dark shadow crossed her heart.

And southward swept the prince and the Highland clans.
        They captured the capital city, Edinburgh,
and nearby at the battle of Prestonpans
        made a laughing stock of Johnny Cope,
                the English General,
by routing the English army as he took to his heels!

> *Hey, Johnnie Cope, are ye waukin' yet?*
> *Or are your drums a-beating yet?*
> *If ye were waukin' I wad wait,*
> *Tae gang tae the coals in the morning.*
>
> *Fye now, Johnnie, get up an' rin,*
> *The Highland bagpipes mak' a din*
> *It's better tae sleep in a hale skin,*
> *For it will be a bluidie mornin'.*

So southwards, taking Edinburgh,
        crossing the border,
                capturing Carlisle,
on to Manchester they marched, as far as Derby.

They were within striking distance of London,
    where the alarmed English king and court
        were preparing to flee across the channel.

> *There is a tide in the affairs of men,*

Which, taken at the flood, leads on to fortune;
Omitted, all the voyage of their life,
Is bound in shallows and in miseries.

For whatever reasons, from Derby they retreated,
   leaving en route, a small garrison in Carlisle.
        In that garrison, the seasoned warrior Fergus
            and his young Maclain clansman, Donald.

The prince's army retreated north
        to the desperate defeat
            on the bleak Drumossie Moor,
                the fateful field of Culloden.

There, on the sixteenth of April in the year 1746,
   on a day of driving sleet and icy wind,
       the English army under the Duke of Cumberland
annihilated the exhausted forces of the Highland army.

And that fateful day
ended the high hopes of the Stewart cause,
destroyed the clan system
and with it, a whole way of life.

Cumberland, by his ruthless atrocities,
   after this battle earned the name,
       'Butcher' Cumberland.
Death, or at least exile,
   were the fates of all those associated
       with the cause of the Bonnie Prince.

Burned were their homes,
Exile and death, scattered the loyal men.

While Cumberland's army marched back southwards,

young Donald and Fergus were in the small garrison
in Carlisle.

This small garrison was easily overcome
by the might of the English cannon fire,
and soon the castle was overcrowded
with Jacobite prisoners,
followers of the prince.

The English government found a swift and inhuman way
of solving this overcrowding:
punitive and exemplary trials were held.
The prisoners were divided into 'lots'
and told to draw straws.

1-2-3-4-5-6   1-2-3-4-5-6

The man who drew the short straw
was tried for treason,
the punishment – death.
The others were exiled to Canada, the New World, America.

Fergus and Donald were in one 'lot'
and the one who drew the short straw
was young Donald.

On the night before his execution
the two sat talking.
'Fergus,' said Donald, who was a piper, 'I've composed a song;
I've been thinking about Mary,
about you, Fergus,
and about Scotland.
You will be taking the high road of exile over the seas.
I will be taking the low road of death,
some call the fairy road,

and I'll be home in Scotland before you.
        You will never see Scotland again
                and I will never see Mary again.
I'd like you to learn my song,
        and maybe one day
                it will win back to Scotland,
mayhap even to Mary.'

And eye to eye, mind to mind, heart to heart,
    Fergus learned the song from young Donald that night
                      and they parted.

Loch Lomond

By yon bonnie banks and by yon bonnie braes
Where the sun shines bright on Loch Lomond,
There me and my true love were ever wont to gae
On the bonnie, bonnie banks of Loch Lomond.

Chorus:
Ye'll tak the high road and I'll tak the low road,
And I'll be in Scotland afore ye,
But me and my true love we'll never meet again
On the bonnie, bonnie banks of Loch Lomond.

O, the wee birdies sing and the wild floo'ers spring
And in sunshine the waters are sleeping,
But the broken heart it kens, nae second spring again
Though the waefu' may cease frae their greetin'.

Chorus

By yon bonnie banks and by yon bonnie braes
Where the sun shines bright on Loch Lomond,
There me and my true love we'll never meet again
On the bonnie, bonnie banks of Loch Lomond.

Chorus

The song made its way back to Scotland and is still sung today, but whether Mary ever heard it, the story doesn't tell.

The Rout of Moy

This is the story of a 'heroic' lady, a prince, a blacksmith, and a great piper. It is the story of Colonel Anne McIntosh, Scotland's beautiful rebel, or as the Bonnie Prince Charlie styled her, 'La Belle Rebelle.' She was a fearless supporter of Charles Edward Stewart in his fight against the English, a fight to put Charles on the throne of Great Britain.

On the night of the sixteenth February 1746, Prince Charles, with a small retinue of followers, visited the House of Moy near Inverness, the home of Lady Anne McIntosh. There the prince had the best of Highland hospitality: ten covered dishes with china and crystal from France, local venison, salmon, fine wine and usquabae – whisky.

The night was merry with conversation and storytelling before the prince and his men retired early to bed.

As a precaution, Lady Anne sent five men, led by Donald Fraser the blacksmith, to watch the Inverness road. It was a night of wind and rain, thunder and lightning. No sooner had the prince gone to bed than there came the sound of running footsteps. Who was this? A young boy, soaked, wrapped in a plaid and gasping for breath as he blurted out his story.

Word of the prince's whereabouts had come to the ears of the English Commander in Inverness, Lord Louden, and he had despatched fifteen hundred men on the fourteen miles to Moy Hall to surprise and capture the prince.

The lad had taken the short route over the hills. Louden's force, to avoid being observed, had taken the longer concealed route along the road. The soldiers of the English Army approached. What chance had five men against a force of fifteen hundred?

In the dark, these five crouched amongst the peat stacks, waiting. The blacksmith, Donald Fraser, had a plan. The five were placed well apart and, on Donald's command, one after another, out of this concealment in the dark, yelled out:

'Clan Chattan, fire!' and discharged a shot,

'Clan McPherson, fire!' – a shot,

'Clan Fergusson, fire!' – a shot,

'Sergeant Ross, fire!' – a shot,

'Sergeant McIntosh, fire!' – a shot.

And in the rain, lightning and thunder, the English concluded that they confronted the entire Jacobite Army and retreated ignominiously to Inverness. This became known as the Rout of Moy, unsurprisingly a favourite tale in the Clan McIntosh history.

There was only one casualty in this Rout of Moy and that was the piper, Donald ban MacCrimmon.

For unknown generations, certainly from the year 1600, the MacCrimmons, based near Dunvegan in Skye, were the hereditary pipers to Clan MacCleod. From that time they were famed far and wide and pipers came to learn their piping at the college of the great MacCrimmon Pipers, to learn the Pibroch, the classical music of the pipers, developed by the MacCrimmon pipers. They paid handsomely to learn.

Story has it that Donald ban MacCrimmon, the last surviving of the seven sons, met a friend who told him, 'Donald, I dreamed a strange dream that I met you, and you going thinner and thinner, and into a black cave you were disappearing.'

Donald, too, had dreamed of his death and it was said that an old woman, a cailleach, heard from the hills the whining and keening of the Banshee, the fairy woman whose cry was a portent of death. Heeding these omens, Donald ban MacCrimmon composed a haunting melody, a lament for himself and for the music of the great College of Piping.

MacCrimmon's Lament

Round Cuillin's peak the mist is sailing
The banshee croons her note of wailing
But my blue e'en wi' sorrow are streaming
For him that will never return – MacCrimmon

No more, no more, no more forever
In war or peace shall return MacCrimmon
No more, no more, no more forever
Shall love or gold bring back MacCrimmon

The breezes on the braes are mournfully moaning
The brook in the hollow is plaintively mourning
But my blue e'en wi' sorrow are streaming
For him that will never return – MacCrimmon

No more, no more, no more forever
In war or peace shall return MacCrimmon
No more, no more, no more forever
Shall love or gold bring back MacCrimmon

Seventeen Coffins

I saw these little wooden two-inch coffins, with figures within, in the National Museum of Scotland, Edinburgh. Discovering several theories about their origin, I invented this version.

Up the close and doon the stair,
Bairnies run fae Burke and Hare.
Burke's the butcher, Hare's the thief,
And Knox is the man wha buys the beef.

In the dark o' mony a nicht
When ain and a' are sleeping,
Through the graveyard by the dyke
There go two shadows creeping.

It was the year 1828. A woman emerged from the trees and the soggy soil onto the slopes of Arthur's Seat. From the pocket in her coat, she took a tiny coffin no longer than her own forefinger. Within it was a tiny doll.

She moved a rock aside and placed it carefully within a little sepulchre beside sixteen other little coffins; each contained a little figure neatly dressed, this last one, a woman. She kneeled down and tears ran from her face.

'Lord God,' she prayed, 'bless, bless all these dead ones. And may the spirit of Mary Docherty be saved so that on the day of judgement her body can rise whole and complete.

Forgive William ... he is not a bad man ...' She burst into tears. 'Forgive me ... I love him ... I love him.'

Helen McDougal was torn apart. The two things she loved were at war. Here on this cold morning hillside she sought absolution. She knew God would raise the dead at the last day. And the man she loved, William Burke, was taking the bodies of people he had killed to the doctors at Surgeons' Hall to be cut up, mutilated.

How could these broken bodies rise on God's judgement day? Maybe God would listen and accept her offer of the perfect little bodies in her coffins so that they could rise whole and complete on the last day. 'Please God, please God ... save these people, save William.'

Ghostly wisps of mist like wraiths curled round the crags. She was dizzy, dizzy remembering the last ceilidh, the one with the old Irish woman, Mary Docherty. With each victim it seemed Burke was more troubled. Screaming in his sleep. Waking with trembling limbs, clinging to her. And after each body for the doctor the ceilidh was wilder, the last, a frenzy. William Burke beating the bodhran, singing, the music bouncing; dancing, singing, drinking ... and at the end of the night, 'Sing, Helen, sing for your Irish sweetheart darlin ... sing me to sleep will ye.' She played on the clarsach she loved for the man she loved and sang:

> *I left my baby lying there,*
> *lying there, lying there,*
> *I left my baby lying there*
> *to go and gather blaeberries.*
>
> *Hovan, hovan, gorrie a go*
> *gorrie a go, gorrie a go,*
> *Hovan, hovan, gorrie a go*
> *Never found my baby o.*

(Highland Fairy Lullaby)

And the nightmare of the morning. The old woman dead under the bed, Mary Docherty. The arrest. The little weasel Hare and his wife Margaret, 'turning king's evidence' they called it. So now these two were free.

Christmas Day 1829. After twenty-four hours, the verdict: 'William Burke, guilty.' The sentence: 'To be hanged by the neck until you are dead and your body to be given over to public dissection.'

She'd never forget the look of William from the dock when he heard the verdict: 'Thank God, you're out of the scrape, Helen.'

And he'd looked at her, one of these looks of his that still seemed to have a little laughter in it. As if he was glad it was all over.

'His body to be given over to public dissection.' She would need one last coffin, for William.

> *But justice aye maun hae her way,*
> *They baith hae got their share.*
> *It's the gallows tree for William Burke*
> *And the pauper's grave for Hare.*

> *Up the close and doon the stair,*
> *Bairnies run fae Burke and Hare.*
> *Burke's the butcher, Hare's the thief,*
> *And Knox is the man wha buys the beef.*

The Twice-Hanged Man

Not only is fact stranger than fiction, but often more horrifying. My tale is such a one, where dark echoes lurk in Edinburgh's medical school at Surgeons' Hall.

There was a time in Edinburgh, known as 'the killing time', notorious for the Edinburgh murderers, Burke and Hare, who killed sixteen people to supply corpses for the dissections carried out by the infamous Dr Knox in that same medical school. This was a time when bodies of hanged criminals were the only legitimate source of bodies to be dissected.

Our story tells of a man whose spirit, they say, still walks the old lecture halls and anatomy rooms of the University of Edinburgh. This man was tried for murdering a victim to sell to the doctors. He was found guilty and sentenced to be hanged – a public hanging in the Grassmarket, a gruesome source of entertainment that attracted large crowds.

The gallows were so shabbily constructed and the whole affair so clumsily handled that when he was 'dropped,' his toes could keep tantalising contact with the stool, so that the crowd watched his macabre dance of death – some laughing, some cheering, but at length the convulsions weakened and ceased and he hung limp, contorted, motionless.

The body was taken over the street to a doctor to be pronounced dead. During the examination the body began to twitch and kick. The doctor then revived the man so that the sentence once more could be enacted, and he was carried across the road to be hanged again.

This time the spectacle was even more macabre, as the hangman hung onto the condemned man, thus lending his weight to the rope. This time the body was pronounced dead and taken to the anatomy halls for dissection.

Now science takes a gruesome hand in our tale. Edinburgh, famed for its medical advances then and still now, raised many moral questions. At that time, in Italy, Galvani had established that attaching a frog to an electrical current from a battery caused it to twitch. This charge was called 'animal electricity.'

Galvani's nephew at that time was in Edinburgh, and in the name of science it was decided to try this 'animal electricity' on a human being. The human being chosen was our twice-hanged man.

The lecture hall, in raked ranks, was full of students. The corpse was placed in a chair in front of the audience and strapped, electric chair-fashion, into position. The electrodes, with crude, jagged clamps, were attached to various parts of the body.

The lecture theatre itself was dimly lit by candles; only the area around the body brightly illuminated. The battery was connected to the leads. The students gazed in silence. The body began to twitch and the young Italian tried to explain why this happened. Some students began to cry for the experiment to be stopped, but the professor calmly announced that this was the expected response.

At that a low, gurgling moan came from the corpse, and the professor stated that this was the effect of the electric agitation on the fluid in the lungs. The students themselves were becoming increasingly agitated and alarmed when the corpse began to jerk and shake, making ever more alarming sounds, and suddenly opened its eyes, gazing back at the horrified audience with a look of distress and pure horror.

Some students screamed, some fainted and one voice cried out, 'Stop! Stop – he is living, he is alive!'

At that moment, the professor walked calmly behind the seated victim and with a scalpel, slit the throat. The young Galvani rushed to disconnect the leads and the fastenings to the chair, and to the disbelief and petrified revulsion of the students, who were by then frozen by the event, the professor moved the corpse to the dissecting table. He made a violent incision across the chest, wrenching the ribs apart, and plunged his hands into the open wound and wrenched out the heart – which, some said, was beating still.

The epilogue to this gruesome tale is that from time to time, in the gloomy halls of anatomy, a ghost walks those halls and passages with a look of anguish and pain and carries in its hands a still-beating heart.

The Harper's Pass

This legend was published in The Bee, *a periodical magazine edited by Dr Anderson and published in Edinburgh in the 1890s. The following is my version, considerably extended by my imagination. The theme, featuring an old harpist and his betrayal in love, makes a moving tale to tell and enhance, if you like with music and song, as I suggest in the text.*

The Eriskay Love Lilt

When I'm lonely, dear white heart,
Black the night or wild the sea.
By love's light my foot finds
The old pathway to thee.

Vair me o, ro van o
Vair me o ro ven ee,
Vair me o ru o ho
Sad am I without thee.

(Marjory Kennedy-Fraser)

The little girl was born on the island of Tiree a long time ago. She was christened Kyla, meaning in the Gaelic tongue '*so beautiful that only poets can describe her.*' And so, it was she grew up to be as her name, a young woman of exquisite beauty, with a lilting, beguiling walk, eyes that laughed and sparkled, the lark's song in her voice. Like the legendary Grainne of the old Celtic tales, it was said that she could awaken in a man 'the terror of a tameless love.' Wherever she went men's eyes and hearts followed her. But to her they were playthings.

She lived on the Island of Tiree with her mother, her father having vanished, no one knew where, when she was a baby. He was said to be the finest of harpers and it was as if her heart followed his music, for wherever there was a fine harper, a ceilidh house, music, she would be there listening. Not listening only, for she repaid her favourites and the beauty of their music with the fierce fire of her passion and the favour of her thighs. After the trembling of the harp strings faded into the night air, she taught them the melodies of desire in the secret dark. Many nights her mother spent alone in the silent house.

One young man, Donald Rua, the red-haired Donald, a wild and handsome wandering harpist, was for a time the very music of her heart. They were well matched in the fickleness of their affections and a strange, powerful bond fastened them until his roving spirit took him and he left the island.

> *Vair me o, ro van o*
> *Vair me o ro ven ee,*
> *Vair me o ru o ho*
> *Sad am I without thee.*

When Kyla's mother died, she heard of the fame of Farquhair McLeod, harper to the Lord of the Isles, and so she crossed to the nearby Island of Mull and there in the halls of Moy Castle she first heard and became captive to the singing harp strings of Farquhair. Farquhair was many years older than she, a seasoned harper celebrated far and wide for his matchless music, heart touching, carrying the voices and whispering mysteries of his people. The music from his fingers on the harp put upon the people a spell of enchantment. His clarsach was old and rare and beautiful. The base strings of gold, the middle of silver and the top of finest brass. The harp was the love of his life. Where he played all over the island, Kyla followed and soon the harpist was ensnared by her beauty and lost in his love for her. In this love he was powerless even though he knew it was a snare he would one day rue. Together they travelled the island, an open door everywhere for the harper's music and his beautiful, young wife.

One morning, bright and crisp in the late autumn of the year, Kyla and Farquhair set out, passing the ancient stone circle of Loch Buie, skirting the shadow of Ben Buie and making their way across the island. Their path lay across a mountain pass – at the best it would be a long day's walking – but as they climbed the bealach in the late afternoon the sky darkened, the weather closed in and a mountain mist, cold and clinging, enveloped them. A fierce, sudden wind hurled daggers of hailstones in their faces as they struggled upwards. Near the summit of the bealach they found a cave and there they rested.

Dark was falling, flurries of snow swirled into the cave, and for all Farquhair held her closer and closer in his arms, his plaid around her, she shuddered and trembled.

'Make a fire, make a fire,' she demanded, and he bent against the howling wind that whined up the corrie, gathered what he could of bracken and wrenched some heather from the hillside but there was little to burn, and Kyla, ghost-pale, complained bitterly.

'Keep me warm, keep me warm,' she said. 'You say you love me, keep me warm.'

In desperation he broke his harp to feed the fire, sacrificing one love of his life to keep the other alive. In this way they survived the night, and as the morning sun lifted the mist, they saw coming up the pass a young man riding a sturdy highland garron.

The young man, seeing the pair huddled and shivering round the embers of the fire, dismounted and passed a flask of whisky from which they both drank. The old harper did not see the unspoken glance of recognition the girl exchanged with the stranger. 'Ride my horse,' he said to Kyla. And so, the three made their way over the pass, Kyla mounted on the stranger's sturdy garron.

Below them in a gully tumbled the river. 'Farquhair,' said the girl, 'a great thirst is on me. Will you get me some water?' The harper scrambled down into the rocky gorge and filled the flask from the rushing stream. When he climbed back with the fresh water, Kyla and the stranger were gone.

Looking down the glen, he saw them hurrying away in the bright mist of morning mounted on the garron together, the stranger with his arms around the girl, holding her as only a lover would.

Farquhair sat on a rock. 'Loisgh mi mo chlàrsach dhi[1] ... I burned my harp for her,' he said. And to this day that phrase is used to express the sorrow and despair of love betrayed, and in Mull that bealach is known as The Harper's Pass.

On Raglan Road of an autumn day, I saw her first and knew
That her dark hair would weave a snare that I would one day rue.
I saw the danger, yet I passed along the enchanted way.
And I said, 'Let grief be a fallen leaf at the dawning of the day.'

('On Raglan Road', Patrick Kavanagh)

---

[1] Phonetically – loschy me mo chlasach ee.

The Blind Piper

A brief outline of a story Duncan Williamson told me he'd heard in Ireland stirred my imagination to compose this adaptation in verse.

This is the story of Tormid.
It takes place on a green island,
    a place where time is told in the tides,
        in the falling of the leaves,
            in the setting of the sun,
                in the rising of the moon.

It is from a green island
    where the spirit is still in the land
        and the little people keep the glitter in all living things;
            in the creatures and birds,
                the flowers and the trees.

There is a legend about that place
    where once were many trees
        and if you find yourself there
            in a cottage on that green island
                you might see standing by the fire
                    a half-burned log.

It is not half-burned by any mortal fire
        but by a mystery
                and the half-burned log has a story.

To the people in times long gone
        wood and trees were sacred.
For the wood held music,
        music was in the trees;
                they whispered and danced and sang.
The people loved the trees.
        They worshipped the trees.
                The trees sang the music of the breeze
                      and the people loved that music.

They heard the melodies in the wind.
        Carried in the breeze, the rhythms and tunes.
And the priests and seanchaidhean of that old time
        and of these ancient people, listened,
                and they learned from the trees.

And then,
   by the mystery of their art,
        they found the music of the trees
            and they took the trees,
                when their life was gone,
they turned them into
        the haunting harps,
            the merry fiddles,
                the whistles and flutes and pipes and drums.

They caught and kept and carried
        the music of the trees
                and the people put their breath
                      through whistle and flute and pipe

and made music
>   like the breeze in the leaves of the trees.
>   >   And the leaves danced.

Now it happened
>   in this long ago time
>   >   that there was an old man,
>   >   >   a wandering piper,
>   >   >   >   and beautiful his music.

His chanter was of the finest wood
>   and when he played, an enchantment fell upon the people.

He said he played the music of the trees.
It was told that his music
>   brought hearing to a deaf young woman
>   >   and from that time, wherever he went, she would go.

And she became his wife.

One thing they longed for was a child,
>   >   a child who would carry on the music.

Then one day the young woman
>   was gathering driftwood by the sea to make a fire.

On the shore was an old and nut-brown woman,
>   a half-blind cailleach.

She was trying to keep her fire alight,
>   scratching around for wood,
>   >   for on it was only one half-burned log.

The young piper's wife gave her half her bundle of sticks.
'Bless you. Bless you,'
>   said the cailleach, 'bless you, child.'

She looked at her:
>   'I see a yearning in your eyes.'

'I have no children,' said the girl. 'More than anything in the world,
>   I wish I had a little boy who could play the music

when Tormid, his father,
    the piper, is gone.'
'Give me your hand. As you wish, so it will be,' said the cailleach.
'A year from this day,
    and by the sea, by your fire,
        there will be a half-burned log,
            like this one here.
You will have your wish, its boon and bane.'

And true to the old cailleach's word,
    at the turn of the year,
        the young woman was carrying a child.
But strange to say,
    as the life grew within the young woman,
        the force of life in the old piper dwindled.

One October evening,
    they set their camp by the shore.
Birth pains came upon the young woman.
The piper lit a fire and tended her
    and the last music the old man heard,
        as he helped her with the birth,
            was the cry of his newborn son.

It was one year to the day
    from the old wife's prophecy
        and on the fire
            was a half-burned log.

She had a son to play the music.
That night her husband did not wake from his sleep.
        Her husband was gone.

She called her little boy Tormid,
    after his father,

and to be sure, he had his father's music.
And more.

He came to be the greatest piper in all the islands,
    in all Scotland and if in all Scotland,
        why, in all the wide world.
Through the set of pipes
    the trees still made their beautiful music
and when Tormid played,
    the flowers closed their eyes,
        the bees stopped their buzzing,
            the birds in the trees stopped singing.
The clouds stood still.
    The little stream stopped running.
        They all listened.
The trees leaned over.
    The blades of grass bent to hear the wonderful music.
The animals.
    The birds.
        The fish in the sea.
            They all listened,
                listened to the beautiful music of Tormid.

Tormid had no home,
    no cottage,
        no village.
For he wandered all over the western islands.
He played his beautiful music for everyone,
    and for his eyes, wherever he went,
        Tormid had his old mother, for Tormid was blind.
For everyone he played his music,
    from the highest to the lowest.
        To Tormid it made no difference.
For lord and lady, in castle and hall,
    for tinkers by their fires,

               for beggars and thieves
                    or milkmaid in the green field,
                         Tormid played for everyone.
And they all welcomed
     blind Tormid and his mother, wherever they travelled,
          for everyone loved the beautiful music
               of the greatest piper in the land,
                    the best piper in all the wide world.

His music was known and loved everywhere,
                and he said, 'It is the music of the trees.'
When he played, the people would dance.
          They would weep.
                The sorest heart would be soothed to sleep.
The clouds stood still.
     The birds stopped singing.
          The bees stopped buzzing.
               The flowers closed their eyes.
                    Even the little streams stopped to listen.

Everyone loved his music.
They gave Tormid and his mother
     food and drink and shelter,
          maybe a cloak for the winter cold,
               or shoes for the hard, long roads they walked.
They loved Tormid,
     the finest piper in all the western islands.
And the half-burned log by the fireside,
     this is in memory of Tormid.

One day, Tormid and his mother
had just left the big house of the laird, high on the hill.
'Time to take the road again, Tormid,' said his mother.
'We've been well wined and dined.
     Time to go.

Time for us to find another place
> for you to play your pipes.'

So on they travelled
> and on they travelled.
>> Down a winding road they walked
>>> by leafy ways and grassy ways.

Down towards the sea they were making their way
when Tormid stopped.
'Mother, I hear music.
> I hear fiddle and flute and the drums,
>> but no pipes can I hear.'
And on they walked and came to a turn in the road
> and there before and below them
>> a fine, flat, grassy field.
A fine, smooth, sandy beach
> and the sea glistening blue in the sun.

On the green and the white,
> the grass and the beach
>> was a great dance.
Folk of all ages dancing and twirling
> to the merry music of flute and fiddle and drum
and into that great dancing place
walked blind Tormid and his old mother.
The dancers and musicians stopped to welcome them,
> Tormid and his mother.

Tormid took out his pipes and began to play.
The people listened.
> Stood and listened.
>> People drifted towards the music of Tormid.
Beasts came down from the hill to listen,
> cattle and horses and sheep.

The clouds stood still.
    The birds stopped singing.
        The flowers closed their eyes
            and the little stream stopped to listen.
They all listened
    to the beautiful music
        played on his set of pipes of wood.
            The music of the trees.
And then Tormid struck up a lively jig
    and old and young danced,
        danced as they had never danced before.
           They danced until they could dance no more.
Even Tormid himself was tired.

The old dancing master, who had been teaching the people, came to Tormid.

'I never heard such fine music, Tormid! Such fine playing! Will you take a dram?'

'Och, that I will,' said Tormid. 'That I surely will.'

'Trouble is, I've no such thing as a glass,' said the dancing master.

'Och, devil the glass!' said blind Tormid. 'Give me the bottle!' And he tilted his head and took,
      not a dram, not a gill, not a half,
          but drained the whole bottle.

'That whisky was not bad!' said he. 'Not bad!'

He stood still.
    He seemed to be listening,
        gazing towards the sea with his blind eyes.
He seemed to be listening, intently listening.
And then he took from his belt
    a little wooden, polished whistle
        and he began to play
as if he was hearing the music himself

and if the music was wonderful before,
>   now there was no word for it.
No one had ever heard such beautiful music beside the sea.
The exhausted people took new life.
>   The old leapt and danced along with the young.
>   >   The crippled along with the nimble.
Even Tormid's old mother swayed to the strange, merry music.
The whole green field was filled with a whirl of dancers
>   and the whole white beach below
>   >   for lobsters and crayfish and crabs
>   crept and crawled from the sea,
>   >   prancing sideways on their claws,
>   >   >   prancing and dancing,
>   >   >   >   capering, cavorting in the sand.
Fish skimmed the waves,
>   flying, twisting, turning in the air.
Great, grey seals rolled and lolled,
>   lunged and lolloped in the sea,
>   >   stumbled and tumbled,
>   >   >   flipped and flopped onto the beach
>   >   >   >   to the rhythm of the strange, unearthly music.
On its eight great legs
>   a gangly octopus clambered ashore
>   >   and danced a gleesome eightsome reel of its very own.
Seabirds flocked to the dance.
Long-legged, haughty herons pirouetted with playful puffins.
Great, grey cormorants
partnered dainty, dapper oyster catchers.
Petite sandpipers bobbed and curtseyed with lofty, cooing curlews.
Waders and divers, gannets and guillemots,
>   gulls of every kind
>   >   pranced and danced on the white beach.

It seemed as if the very sea was singing.
　　　The waves in little ripples, moving to the tides of music
and Tormid, gazing seaward with blind eyes
　　　　played as he had never played
　　　　　　on his little wooden whistle,
and then wafting through the water like a wave,
　　　came swaying a beautiful woman,
　　　　　　swaying through the water towards the shore.
Her hair a shimmering sheen of gold and green,
　　　pale as the breaking wave her skin,
　　　　　white as pearl her teeth,
　　　　　　　coral her lips.
A flowing glow of white and green and blue, her gown.
　　　Ribbons of seaweed,
　　　　　a necklace of amber and jewels in her hair
and swaying, swaying,
　　　she sang through the waves.
　　　　　　Her voice sweeter than any music.
Clear across the water she sang the name, 'Tormid.'
The people were struck dumb, as if enchanted.
All the animals,
　　　all the people,
　　　　　all the creatures of the sea stood still as stones,
　　　　　　　on the green field, the white sands.

In the sea she swayed,
　　　danced to the wonderful music,
　　　　　swayed through the waves towards the shore,
　　　　　　　towards Tormid
and her song was wild and sweet and full of yearning,
　　　　full of longing.

Over the water it rippled,
　　'Tormid, Tormid, come with me
and I will be your bride of the sea.'

Through the water she danced towards the music.
> The beautiful music of Tormid
on his little shiny whistle.
'Tormid!' his mother cried.
> 'It is a sea witch! Do not go!
>> Your music is of the earth and rivers and the trees.'

Every creature was motionless and silent.
No sound but the music
> and in it the strange song of the sea maiden.
Softly she sang. 'It is no music of the earth you play
but of the caverns of the sea.
My father's palace is under the waves where he is king,
come play for him.
It is the singing of the tide you play.'
Only his music and her voice in the silence.
'Come, Tormid. Come to me, and I will be your bride of the sea.'
And Tormid began to walk blindly towards the sea,
towards the sea maiden.

'Tormid, my son! My son, do not go!
> You are the king of pipers.
>> Your music is not of the sea, it is of the earth.
>>> It is of the trees.'

'It is the music of the sea,' sang the sea maiden.
She danced, she swayed,
   softly she sang, 'Come, Tormid, be my king
and I will be your bride.'

And Tormid moved towards her sweet, soft song into the sea,
played all the time the sea music on his sparkling whistle.
'She will destroy you!' his mother howled.

The music filled the air.

The maiden lured him with her soft, sweet voice
and he danced into the sea.
His mother fell on her knees, wailing his name.
Tormid stopped playing and turned his blind eyes once more
to the shore.
'I must go,' he said.
The people were bewitched.
'I shall send you a token, Mother, of my music,
        the music of the trees.
                You will remember it, Mother.
                      You will remember it.'

And then the sea maiden put her arms around him.
        Her singing ceased
                and they were gone under the waves into the sea.
                        Tormid, the blind piper and the sea maiden.

The animals returned to the hill to graze.
The crabs and lobsters and sea creatures
                slipped back into the water.
The birds flew into the sky.
The flowers opened their leaves.
The people turned homeward.
The green field was empty.
        Empty.
        The white beach.
And as dark fell
        the shore was deserted but for one old, white-haired woman,
                weeping and gazing
                        always towards the sea.

The local people took care of the old woman.
Every morning she went to the sea's edge and waited for the tide.
The weeks stretched to months

and a year all but a day passed
and on the shore one cold morning,
> she knelt down and gazed out to sea.

There an old fisherman found her kneeling,
> cold, gazing with blind eyes towards the sea,
>> cold in death
and riding on the incoming tide and washed on to the shore
> the fisherman saw a mystery,

a log,
  a still-burning log,
    a log and a sign she never saw.

The old fisherman kept that log and put it by his fire.
The villagers buried the old woman in the little cemetery by the sea.
And so the log is in remembrance of blind Tormid
and the music from the trees.
And they do say that each year,
> a burned log comes ashore on the tide,
>> the token promised to his mother by blind Tormid.

So you will know that if you are in a cottage,
> and a half-burned log rests by the fire,
>> it is for the love of the trees and their music
and remembrance of the greatest piper in all the western islands,
> blind Tormid.

And they do say that if you pass by a certain way
> you can some days hear
the sound of the pipes by the sea,
> the piping of blind Tormid.

But be advised.
> If you hear a tune from the depths of the sea,

>   do not go diving down to find blind Tormid.
> And if a sea maiden comes from the waves
>   to speak with you or sings,
>   bow politely and come away.
>
> And, don't swallow a bottle of whisky at one go,
>   it will do you no good at all!

The Coo That Ate the Piper

This was another story told to me by the wonderful old Travelling man, Willie McPhee, who was a piper, a kenspeckle figure standing in kilt and regalia on the layby on the road to Glencoe. A real gentleman of the road, he had lived in tents and caravans more or less all of his life and was a welcome singer and storyteller at the Scottish Storytelling Centre.

One night, in my flat in Dundas Street, he told me this story. He said, 'David, there's many strange things happen, and I'll tell you this, David, this to me was one of the strangest. One night, it was a cold night, it was a winter's night and I think it was more or less near New Year, and I was walking along and I thought, "I need to get a wee bit of shelter, I need to get a bite to eat at least, that's what I'll do," and so I came across this farmhouse and I went up and knocked on the door. To my surprise, there came to the door my friend Hamish, another Traveller. I said, "Hamish, what are you doing in this house?" Hamish said, "Och, Willie, this house is mine." I said, "This can't be your house, you've never had a house in your life. You've been on the road all your life, you've been living in tents, you've been living like me." Hamish said, "Willie, this is my house. Come in." Well, I was very uncertain, but it seemed nobody else was there, and I could hear a warm fire crackling and it was a cold night, so

I thought, "Alright, I'll just go in." So I went in and Hamish said, "Have a wee smoke." So I took out my pipe, settled down,' and this is the story that Hamish told Willie.

'Now Hamish too was a piper, and he said, "Now Willie, it was a year to the day this happened to me. I was walking the road, I had my pipes and it was early in the evening. It was New Year's Eve and I knew I would get a good welcome at this hotel in the village.

I rang the bell and right enough the proprietor himself, a good man who always welcomed me, came and said, 'Oh, there you are, Hamish the piper.'

'Yes,' I said, 'I was wondering if you had a little bite to eat.'

'You're most welcome tonight, Hamish. We've got a lot of guests here from Germany and France and America, and the piper who was supposed to be coming isn't well so you're most welcome.' So right enough I was welcomed in, given a bite to eat and then took out my pipes and aye, I played bonny. The guests were delighted. I set afoot a few dances, jigs and reels and all the rest, and the evening flew by.

The bells came, people drank in the New Year, it was very merry and jolly. The time was passing by and there was a bit of moon in the sky and it seemed as though a wind had got up, but the proprietor said, 'Hamish, Hamish, I really wish I could give you a bed for the night, but there's nothing – all the places are taken. There's not a space. I'm really sorry, Hamish. But here …'

And he handed me five pounds, a lot of money in these days.

'Thank you, I'll find a place, I always find a place, it's no problem for me.'

But, when I came out, there were flurries of snow; it had been snowing heavily and there was now a deep layer of snow on the ground. And so I was tramping on through the snow and thinking 'Well, this is worse than I thought it would be.' The problem was that I'd walked many a mile and I suddenly realised my boots were leaking and my feet were getting cold. I thought, 'My Lord, on a night like this, I could freeze.' I suddenly tripped over something. I thought maybe a log. Now I was very handy and I thought, 'I'll have a look at this.' And so I began to brush the snow off one end of the log but, to my surprise, it wasn't a log ... it was the frozen face of a dead man.

'Poor soul,' I thought, 'you're not going to see this world again.' He was frozen hard. I brushed off the rest of the snow and saw the fellow was well dressed. He was wearing the most beautiful pair of boots – very, very beautiful boots. I looked at them and thought, 'These boots look to be about my size. I'll just take these boots. I'm sure they'll do the trick. This fellow has no more need of them.'

But, when I started to pull the boots off, they wouldn't budge. Like the rest of the body, they were frozen on and so there was no way I could get them off. But, being a Travelling man, being a bit of a craftsman as well, I always travelled with a few tools and I happened to have a hacksaw in my pack. I thought, 'Well, I can't get the boots, so I'll just take the boots with the feet in them.' So I began to saw and after a while, right enough, one of the boots came off. Of course, the foot was still in it. And then I did the same with the second. Off it came, so now I had the two boots, but I had the two feet in them as well, so I thought, 'Well, I'll just put these in my bag and maybe I'll get them thawed out sometime.'

So I hirpled along because my feet were freezing cold and sore, and then by good fortune I saw a farmhouse. 'Oh,' I thought, 'here we are, I'll maybe get a wee bit of shelter in this place.' I was beginning to get a wee bit hungry too. So I came up to the door and knocked. It was opened by a gruff looking farmer.

'Excuse me, sir,' I said.

'Out of here! We don't want you dirty tykes here.'

And he slammed the door in my face.

'This is not good at all,' I thought, 'I can't spend the night like this outside, I won't survive. I'll end up a corpse like that old fella.' So I took a bit of courage and knocked on the door again, and this time the farmer's wife answered it.

'Excuse me,' I said, 'it's a cold, cold night. I just need a little place to lay my head, that's all.'

And the farmer's wife said, 'You can use the barn, you can sleep in the barn.'

So I said, 'Thank you, thank you very much.'

So off I went to the barn. I found I wasn't the only occupant – there was also old Mavis the cow. She was in her stall and she was nice and warm. So I settled myself down beside her and I watched the cow chewing the cud. I looked at the cow and I saw that down her nostrils were coming two little jets of steam. I thought to myself, 'That's going to be warm, that steam's going to be warm. Maybe this will be my saviour altogether.'

So I took the boots out of my bag and laid them in front of the cow where it was breathing out warm air. Then just near the cow, in the warmth, I fell asleep.

After some time – it was a nice moonlit night and there was a wee bit of light filtering in – I woke and thought, 'Oh, my boots.' And I looked and right enough, with the breath of the cow, they'd melted. So I took one of the boots, took a hold of the ankle and pulled out the foot. Now I had one boot. Same thing with the other. I took it out. 'These boots are going to be warm now,' I thought. So I took off my old boots. Well, they were so old, they just about fell off my feet, and I put my feet in these new boots. Oh, they were comfortable, very, very comfortable and warm foreby.

Then I had this wee bit of a daft idea. 'I know what I'll do, I'll put the feet in my old boots.' So I laid the boots just where the cow was and slipped the feet into them, and then I went to sleep in the next stall, a deep, peaceful sleep.

And the next thing I knew there was this terrible scream. It was the farmer's wife. She'd come into the byre to milk the cow. She was sitting there milking the cow, when suddenly she saw them – the boots, with the feet sticking out of them. So she ran to the farmhouse.

'Husband, husband, a terrible thing has happened!'

He said, 'What do you mean?'

She said, 'The cow has ate the piper!'

'Nonsense,' he said, 'cows is vegetarians.'

She said, 'Well, this one's not. It's ate the piper.'

He said, 'Nonsense.'

She said, 'Come and see for yourself.'

So they went into the byre and the farmer looked ... Argh! Right enough, there was the boots with the ankles sticking out as if they'd been chewed down, and the cow looking very contented. The farmer said, 'We don't want the police to hear about this. I know what we'll do.'

'What'll we do?' she asked.

'We'll bury the boots,' he said.

So out they went. And meantime, of course, I could hear all this.

'We'll bury them under the yew tree,' said the farmer, 'there's no snow there.'

So off they went through the snow and dug a hole and buried the boots.

'There,' said the farmer, 'that's it, nobody will know any the better. That'll be the last we hear of that old piper man, that old tinker.'

But I followed them and was lurking nearby behind a bush. When I heard this, I pulled out my pipes and began to tune them up. As you know, they make an awful squealing and groaning.

'What's that? What's that?' cried the farmer and his wife. Now the morning was misty so I came walking through the mist, blowing my pipes.

'Oh, my God, it's the ghost of the piper!'

And off they ran, through the yard, down the road and out of sight as if they were pursued by the Devil himself."

"So," Hamish said, "that's the way, Willie, that I got this house. Will you have a cup of tea?"' So, Willie took a cup of tea. And that's the story Hamish told Willie, and that's the story Willie told me and that's the story I'm telling you.

The Trowie Wedding

I heard the story first from that fine Shetland storyteller, George Petersen.

This story takes us north of Scotland over the stormy, stormy Pentland Firth, past the islands of Orkney on to bleak Shetland itself. Now Shetland, although in some ways bleak is in other ways warm and extraordinary, and one of the extraordinary things in Shetland is the music of the fiddlers. Oh, the fiddlers play the sweetest of music in Shetland and there isn't a house but used to have a fiddle hanging on the wall. The other thing about Shetland is, if you are not careful, a sea mist or 'haar' will come creeping in over the sea and steal upon you before know it.

The other thing about Shetland is that it has its own brand of little people. Not elves or fairies, but the little trowie people. They have stubby noses, chubby cheeks like red apples and hair carrot-red or black. They are about knee height and they can creep out of that haar, like the mist itself. As you will hear, the trowies have a special love of fiddlers and fiddle music. Our story is about a fiddler, Ranald Eunson.

Now Ranald Eunson was a young man, a Viking, blond hair, beautiful blue eyes and Ranald Eunson was in demand everywhere. At every christening, wedding, wake or celebration, there he was playing his fiddle. And Ranald Eunson was ten days married. Ten days he was married to a very beautiful young woman called Janet.

Janet said to him one day, 'Well Ranald, what are you doing today?'

He said, 'I'm going to be playing at a wedding.'

'Oh,' she said, 'playing at a wedding, well, will you be home for thy supper?'

He said, 'Oh, I could.'

She said, 'I'm making leek and tattie soup.'

'Oooh,' he said, 'leek and tattie soup, that is my favourite soup. I will not fail to be home for my supper.'

'Ranald,' she said, 'you know the weddings, there will be the fiddle playing, there will be the dancing, there will be the singing, there will be the song, there will be the redding up kin, there will be every kind of pleasantry at the wedding. Are you sure you will be home?'

'Oh,' he said, 'if it is leek and tattie soup my dear little one,' he said, 'I will be home. I will not fail thee.'

'Very well,' she said, 'remember the soup will be ready for thy supper.'

And so off he went and out he went and he came along to the wedding house. And oh, of course it was the usual, the whisky was flowing, the conversation was flowing, the redding up kin, the catching up with relations, all this sort of thing and then he was playing. He was playing fiddle tunes, Shetland tunes, Scottish tunes and tunes that other people had never heard. People were dancing, dancing the night away, until at last the lady of the house came and said, 'Ranald, thu wilt stay for thy supper?'

'Oh,' he said, 'thank you, I will stay ... ooh, I'm sorry, I cannot stay for supper on this occasion. I have promised my good lady, my new wife, that I will be home for she's making leek and tattie soup, it's my favourite.'

'Oh very well, don't fail the next time,' she said.

So Ranald tucked his good fiddle under his arm and out he went. And when he went out, coming in from the sea was the cold sea mist, the haar. As he walked along, suddenly he was surrounded by hundreds of the little people, all just about up to his knees, and he looked down and there was one gruff looking little man with a long, white beard who said to him, 'Thu art Ranald Eunson?'

'Oh,' he said, 'indeed I am Ranald Eunson.'

The little man said, 'Thu art a fiddler?'

'Oh,' he said, 'indeed I am a fiddler.'

'Thu hast been playing at the wedding?'

'Oh, you know everything about me, indeed I was playing at a wedding.'

'Well,' said the little man, 'thu know'st that a wedding is no wedding without a fiddler?'

'Oh, of course I know that.'

The little man looked very sad and he said, 'Ranald Eunson, we are having a little trowie wedding, a peerie little wedding with no fiddler, would thu come and play us a tune?'

'Oh,' said Ranald Eunson, 'I would love to do that, but, I promised to go home for leek and tattie soup tonight.'

The little man said, 'Ranald, thu knowst it is no wedding without a fiddle tune. Could thu not come and play a peerie, peerie little tune at a trowie wedding?'

'Very well,' said Ranald. 'I will come and play one peerie tune.'

And at that, there was a horse, a white mare, standing in front of him and three little men helped him up. Hup! hup! hup! and he was on the horse and they were going through the mist and the mist broke ahead as fast as it gathered behind and in no time they came to a wonderful hillside and the little man looked at the hillside and there was a cave and the little man beckoned and said, 'Now follow us.'

Ranald followed and there were teeny weeny little candles no bigger than your little pinkie. He went down these passages and tunnels and labyrinths and they came to a great big hall. There in the hall were hundreds of these little trowie men and women all looking to the front and there was a man looking as if he was dressed as a priest and in front a little lady in a grass-green dress and a little man in a slate-grey suit.

The little priest was saying, 'And I do now pronounce thee, trowie man and trowie wife.'

At that moment the two gave each other such a big, smacking kiss that it reverberated through the whole cave. Everybody cheered.

Then, 'Now, Ranald Eunson,' said the priest man, 'play thy fiddle.'

Oh, and when Ranald took his fiddle, jigs, strathspeys, reels and every kind of dance you can think of in Shetland, dances you've never even heard of. Ranald found his fingers playing like little electric sparks, music he'd never thought or heard of, and the little people were dancing and the more they danced the better he played, and the better he played the better they danced, and it was like the merry dancers in the sky. It was so beautiful. Then in the end the little trowie man came up and he was huffing and puffing in little trowie puffs and he said, 'Oh, Ranald, thank thee, that is enough.'

Ranald said, 'Indeed that is enough. I think it is about time for me going home for my leek and tattie soup.'

The little man looked at him. He said, 'Ranald, we have no white money nor no yellow money to give you. No gold nor silver, I'm sorry.'

Ranald looked at him and said, 'Oh, thy dancing and thy joy was enough. It is payment enough for me.'

The little man looked at him very close and he said, 'Ranald, I can prophesy, and I prophesy this: thy beautiful wife Janet and thee are going to have four little bairnies.'

'Oh,' said Ranald, 'four little bairnies, that's lovely.'

And then the little man said, 'You'll have four more little bairnies.'

'Oh,' Ranald said, 'eight little bairnies.'

Then the little trowie man said, stroking his beard, 'And I

will tell you something. Thy first bairnie will be a little girl.'

'Oh,' said Ranald, 'that's lovely, a little girl, I'd love a little girl.'

The little man looked serious and said, 'But, that little girl will come into the world girning and greeting and howling and yelling and squalling and squealing. The loudest little girl ever born in the Shetland Isles.'

Oh,' said Ranald, 'that's terrible.'

'Like a tempest,' the little man said.

'That's awful,' said Ranald.

'Yes, the little one that you will have next will be a little boy.'

'Oh, a little boy? That's lovely, lovely.' Ranald rubbed his hands. 'Oh, that's very nice.'

The little man looked at him and said, 'No, if that little girl was bad, this little boy will be worse. He will come greeting and howling and yelling and squealing into the world. His voice will be heard as far as the Skagerrak in Sweden.'

'Oh,' said Ranald, 'that's terrible.'

'But,' said the little trowie man, 'I think I could pay thee something that would do thee well.'

'What is that?'

'Come close,' said the little man, 'come close.' And Ranald bent down. 'No, no, come closer,' said the little trowie man. Ranald bent a little closer. The little man made a funny little sound and the funny little sound the man made was the tune of the Fetlar lullaby.

'Hast thu heard that?' the little man asked Ranald.

'Oh, I heard it.'

'Hast thu that in thy head?'

'Oh,' said Ranald, 'I'm a fiddler. If I hear a tune I don't forget it.'

'Very well,' said the little man, 'now it is time to go.'

He made a little beckoning gesture and all the little men ran up the little tunnels and the little passages and Ranald walked behind them and the candles now were burnt down till they were nearly gone. They got outside and there once more was the beautiful white mare. Once more the three little men said, 'Hup, hup, hup!' and up he was on the mare and the mist broke in front as fast as it gathered behind and he plunged through the mist and in no time at all it seemed he arrived right outside his own little stone house.

The little man said, 'Get down.'

The three little men took him down, 'Hup, hup, hup!' Down he came and then the little man said, 'Well Ranald, now farewell, don't forget that tune.'

'Oh,' said Ranald, 'no, I won't forget this night either.' There was a little sound and when Ranald looked again the mare was gone, the little people were gone too.

'Oh,' Ranald said to himself, 'my leek and tattie soup.' He went into the house and when he went in, there sitting by the fire was Janet and she turned on him a look that would have frozen a summer pool.

'Where hast thu been?' she asked.

'I have been playing at a little wedding,' he said. 'Where is my soup?'

'Thy soup is on the table,' she said.

'Oh,' he said, 'lovely.'

He went across and he took his spoon. Oooh, it was cold, it was slimy, it was maggoty, it was stinking.

Ranald Eunson said, 'This is no soup!'

His wife said, 'That was soup fourteen days ago when thu left the house. Where hast thu been?'

He said, 'I was playing at the wedding.'

She said, 'I spoke with the people at the wedding, I asked where you were, I thought you were dead, I thought you were press-ganged, I thought you were murdered. Where wast thu?'

He said, 'I was at the wedd ... oooh, I did but play at a trowie wedding, in the hillside.'

'Oh,' she said and she came forward and threw her arms round his neck and she said, 'Ranald, thu hast come back.'

He said, 'Of course I have come back.'

She said, 'Oh, but people taken by the trowies have been gone for fourteen, twenty one, forty nine years. They have let you come back. I will make you leek and tattie soup till the end of time.'

Oh, I don't know if she did that or not but I know this: when their first little barnie was born it was a little girl, girning and greeting and howling and yelling and squalling and squealing. And Ranald took out his fiddle and played the Fetlar lullaby. Like an angel the little one went to sleep. When Ranald wasn't at home Janet, who was a clever woman, would make up little words to the song and she would sing:

> *Husha-baa Mam's peerie flooer;*
> *Sleep o sleep come ta dee shön.*
> *Mam sall watch dee ooer be ooer*
> *Till dy boannie sleep is döne.*
> *Till dy boannie sleep is döne,*
> *Till dy boannie sleep is döne,*
> *Mam sall watch dee ooer be ooer*
> *Till dy boannie sleep is döne.*

That peerie trowie lullaby taken from the cave of the trowie people is still sung in Shetland today, and when it is sung the bairnies go to sleep like angels.

Jimmy Allen

My friend David Bathgate gave me a wonderful dancing doll he had made. I have clad it in kilt, tartan waistcoat, green knee length socks and red shoes. The doll is made to dance by being suspended by a rod in its back to skim the board on which I set it, its feet just touching the board.

I play the mouth organ which is attached by a frame held in place from behind my head. By adroitly suspending the doll's feet just touching the board it can be made to dance by my tapping the board with my hand to the beat of the music. The tune 'Jimmy Allen' gave its name to this wondrous puppet.

My friend Alison Millen and I created this story while we walked a short distance from Stockbridge to my house in Dundas Street, Edinburgh.

The story / performance is hugely popular with children.

Our story today takes us back to a little village in the West Highlands of Scotland. In the village square was the church, one hotel and one shop. All the cottages were spread along the one main street. At the end of the street standing apart from the other houses lived an ill-tempered man known to the children as The Grump. He never had a smile on his face, nor a kind word to say to anyone. Every day, usually in the afternoon, he would walk along the village street, round the village square and back to his house. He would greet no one as he passed by.

Now round his house was a wall, a high wall which enclosed a beautiful garden. Just outside the wall was a fine, grassy field where the children would play; their favourite game was football, and of course from time to time someone would kick the ball over the wall into the old man's garden. At once he would come rushing out of his house, shake his fist and say, 'Your headmaster, your parents, the village policeman will hear about this!'

The children would not see that ball again. It was added to the collection of footballs the old man had confiscated. He must have had more footballs than flowers.

One day a strange thing happened in the life of the old man. At that time, he was sitting alone in his house as usual, smoking on his little pipe, when there came a knock, knock, knock on his door. This was unusual. He never had any visitors and so his first thought was, 'Who's that knocking at my door? What do they want?' He put down his pipe, got up and went to his door. When he opened it, there standing on his doorstep was an old woman, surely a tinker, one of the Travelling people. Round her shoulders she had a plaid. She wore a long skirt and carried a big basket. In the basket were laces, rattles made from bent bamboo with a bottle top inside, heather scrubbers and other trinkets.

'Sir,' she said, 'something in my basket that you would like to buy today?'

He looked at her. 'There's nothing I'd like to buy from the likes of you. I don't want your sort coming to my door and pestering me. Off with you.' And he slammed the door in her face. The old woman simply turned and left.

Ill-tempered after this interruption to his day, the old man decided it was time to go for his walk. He put on his jacket and his cap, laid down his pipe and opened his door to go outside. On the doorstep was a pair of shoes, wooden shoes, beautiful shoes. 'Hah,' he thought to himself, 'finders, keepers, losers, weepers, now these shoes are mine!' He was surprised at how beautifully they were made of wood. There and then he unlaced his boots, took them off and slipped his feet into these shoes of wood, and did they not fit like silken gloves?

They were the most beautiful, the most comfortable shoes he had ever put on his feet. As he walked down the village street a curious thing began to happen. He felt better, he felt happier; there was a new lightness in his step.

When he reached the village square, a band of musicians was playing a tune. Some of the villagers stood listening.

Then a strange thing happened. The old grump's feet began to make little hop, skip, jumping steps, wonderfully rhythmic dancing steps. A smile no one had ever seen before transformed the old man's face; his arms swung round in great circles as he skipped up and down. He was filled with joy, dancing. It was if the shoes had a life of their own.

When the musicians had finished their tune and the sound died away, everyone applauded the band and the dance of the old man.

The old man couldn't believe it himself. He was smiling; he was happy. He turned to the bandleader and said, 'What is the name of that tune?'

'We just made up this tune, but we won't forget it now! It put a wonderful dance into your feet. What is your name?'

'Jimmy Allen. My name is Jimmy Allen.'

'Well, we'll call the tune Jimmy Allen.'

And so they did. Once more everyone clapped.

From that day Jimmy Allen was a changed man. His mouth no longer drooped down but always had a mischievous smile.

The village children didn't know this. Next day there they were on the beautiful field of green grass outside the high wall

JIMMY ALLEN

round Jimmy Allen's garden and, oops, someone kicked the ball and over the high wall it sailed.

The team looked on in horror when, above the wall, appeared the head of Jimmy Allen, laughing! What was he going to do? The police, the headmaster, their parents?

'Who kicked that ball into my garden?'

'It was me, sir! Sorry, sir!'

'What's your name?'

'D... D... Donald, Sir, Donald Campbell, sir.'

'Very well, Donald Campbell.'

And to everyone's amazement, Jimmy Allen took the ball, threw it into the air and headed it straight into the arms of Donald Campbell. Donald caught it!

'That's for you, Donald. Any of your friends like a football?'

A few surprised hands rose. Jimmy Allen headed and kicked ball after ball over the wall until every boy and girl had a ball from his huge stack.

'Come back tomorrow! I'll tell you a story.'

That is just what he did. He told them the sad story of why he had become a grump, but that is a tale for another day.

What did happen was that after their daily football game he invited the team into his beautiful garden or his house. He became their storyteller, their greatest friend. Like a grandpa, he enchanted them with his stories.

As time passed, Donald Campbell became his greatest friend. When Donald got married and had a little girl, Mary, Jimmy was proud to be her godfather.

When Mary was three, a sad thing happened. She had an accident and could no longer walk. Jimmy used to come and tell her stories and try to get her to smile or laugh. But to no avail. She seemed to be made of sadness.

Then one day when Jimmy was trying to cheer her up, who should pass by but the village band, and what should they be playing but Jimmy Allen's old tune. As soon as the music started, Jimmy began to do his funny little dance: first one foot would flick the ground then each foot, he would skip up and down and his arms began to whirl around, one after the other.

Mary began to laugh. She laughed and laughed.

From that time, when Mary was sad, Jimmy did his little dance. Then she listened to his stories. Jimmy was her best friend.

Years rolled by and at last Jimmy was a very old man. It came to his ninety-fifth birthday; the villagers decided to hold a celebration for Jimmy. It happened that this very day was the anniversary of when Jimmy had got his wonderful shoes. The hall was packed. This was to be the greatest ceilidh, birthday party of all!

'Jimmy,' said Donald Campbell. 'Here is your birthday cake, ninety-five candles. Can you blow them out?'

Jimmy took a huge breath, leaned over the cake, took the biggest breath ever and blew, blew every candle out. Everyone applauded and cheered.

'Do you have a birthday wish Jimmy?'

He scratched his old head and said, 'The day I got these shoes, I changed as if by magic. I got them from an old Travelling woman. I wonder if the band would play the tune that they gave my name?'

'Will you do your little dance?'

'Well if you play nice and slow, I'll try.'

So the band struck up and Jimmy began to dance. Everybody was watching Jimmy's dance, and Mary was laughing. Her eyes were sparkling. His legs were going up and down, his arms started to whirl round and round, everybody began to clap in time. And then suddenly Jimmy stuttered and staggered and he fell on the floor. The music stopped.

People ran across, they loosened his collar. One felt for his pulse, another said, 'Give him the kiss of life.'

Someone asked, 'Is he breathing?'

JIMMY ALLEN

Jimmy Allen was gone!

A great sadness fell upon the village. What were they going to do? They talked about it. One of them said, 'Let's build a statue on the hill for him, shall we?'

'Och no, he wasn't the kind of man that would like a statue,' said someone else.

Then someone suggested, 'Hey Donald you're a carpenter, a wood worker, a carver, aren't you? Do you remember the story of Pinocchio?'

'Aye,' said Donald.

'Remember how the little wooden fella came to life?'

'Yes,' he said.

'Maybe you could make a little doll or something out of these amazing shoes that Jimmy had and maybe you could give that to Mary 'cause Mary was his great favourite.'

And so Donald did. He made a beautiful doll. It looked a little bit like Jimmy Allen. It had legs that were long and dangly. Arms that were long and dangly.

Mary used to sit all alone with this beautiful, little doll. And she used to think, 'Oh, if only, if only Jimmy Allen were alive again.'

And then one day a most extraordinary thing happened.

She was sitting with her little doll and outside the window who should come by but one of the village musicians, playing his little whistle. And the tune he was playing was 'Jimmy Allen'.

As she sat there looking at the little doll, the doll's feet began to move in time to the music. He began to do a little dance. His arms began to swing round.

'Daddy,' she said, 'Daddy, look, Jimmy Allen is dancing again! Oh Daddy look at that. Jimmy Allen is dancing to his music.'

And from that time on whenever that tune was played Jimmy Allen would bounce into life and it put a smile back on Mary's face.

And that is how Jimmy Allen came back to life. In the dancing doll.

Savourna

This is my adaptation of 'The Weeping Girl at the Dancing Place' that I read in 'Twelve Great Black Cats', a book of eerie Scottish tales collected by Sorche nic Leodhas. This is my favourite ghost story. I've always loved stories of the supernatural and, aged twelve, I used to tell them after dark in a disused quarry in the Fairmilehead district of Edinburgh where our gang of friends met.

It is a long time ago, a long time, but among the people in a Scottish Highland glen the story is not forgotten, the story of a girl and her tears and the warning of the cailleachs, the old women.

It was a windy night of harvest time, night of the moon of the ripening of the barley. The crops and oats were gathered in the little glen. Old and young had been in the fields cutting and gathering the ripe grain, the grain that would keep the people and the beasts from hunger through the long winter. Soon the barley would be malted, brewed and distilled into the blessed water of life, the golden whisky to warm the long dark evenings in story, music and song in the ceilidh house.

On this night of the full moon, the moon of the ripening of the barley, it was a time for rejoicing.

Across the face of this bright moon drifted heavy clouds, the dark shadows shifting like weary ghosts over mountain and glen, but the hearts of the young folks were light and easy and heedless of the moody skies. This was a night for revelry and for dancing.

The dancing place was where three rivers met. To this piece of ground, pounded hard and even by generations of dancers, down the glens came the young harvesters. In little, laughing companies, in twos and threes, on foot or sturdy Highland garrons, they came to make merry, to dance their gratitude for the earth's abundance, for another winter's provisions and for work well done.

Often it was the music of pipe or fiddle that put fleetness to their feet in jig, strathspey, reels or dances from the older times. But tonight it was to the puirt-a-beul, the mouth music, that their feet thrummed on the ground as they whirled and set and linked and laughed under the scudding clouds.

One alone did not join them but sat apart weeping. For each of seven years she had come to sit and watch and weep and remember – Savourna. Long, dark hair covering her pale face, she huddled by the tree remembering when she too had danced with her handsome sailor sweetheart. Under this same moon of the harvest they had danced and laughed and linked arms and walked home through the bright moon night planning their wedding.

Then the news had come to their clachan that he was drowned, his body washed ashore and buried in a distant place. It grieved her the more deeply that she could not even weep at his graveside.

From that time no laughter was in her and she never again danced. In dreams she knelt by his graveside in that place without a name by the side of the sea and woke, her pillow drenched with tears.

'Cease yer tears; let his spirit rest. Let him be,' warned the old women, but like a pale ghost she passed her days remembering, remembering, remembering.

'Let him rest in peace,' the cailleachs cautioned, but she drenched the nights in tears.

And each harvest time she came to this place and watched and wept, remembered how they too had laughed and danced. Here each year she relived their last dance, rekindled her grief until the bright pain salted her eyes. While the harvesters danced and laughed under the pleasant face of the moon, she wept.

This was the seventh year of her mourning and weeping. The dancers danced, and as the night wore on, blowy clouds whirled past the moon flinging grey shadows across the dancing place like great, capering ghosts. In a joyous circle the dancers leapt and whirled and spun.

At midnight, out of the shadows of the steepest glen, came a rider. A man in black, on a black horse, a black stallion. He dismounted at the dancing place, threw off his coat and tethered his steed to a branch of the rowan tree giving the weeping girl not a glance.

The dancers, as was the custom of their people, made room in the circle to welcome the stranger. It was as if a wind stole down the glen. A sudden chill quickened the dancers and round and round they flew under the gathering shadows of clouds. On and on through the night they danced, impelled by the stranger's fierce energy until, exhausted, one by one they dropped from the circle and made their ways in little bands down through the glens homewards.

At last only the stranger remained and the girl huddled by the rowan tree. He walked over and stood above her. A slant of moonlight, like a sheen of scraped lead, shone that moment on her face giving it a pallor of one already dead.

'Dance with me,' said the stranger.

'I dance with no one,' Savourna replied.

'Your tears mar your bonnie looks,' he said.

'My tears are for my dead love,' said she.

'Greetin' and grievin' winna bring back the dead,' said he. 'Dance!'

'I will never dance again.'

'Your tears gi'e him nae comfort, nae rest,' said he and seized her by the wrist and pulled her onto the dancing place. And then, as if in the thrall of some inaudible music, round they whirled, alone in the dancing place beneath the scurrying clouds under the pallor of the moon. Through the blur of her tears she looked up into the face of the stranger.

'They told me you were dead,' she whispered.

'Said they so?' said he and on they danced.

'They said that you were drowned.'

'Drowned,' said he and round they whirled.

'In a far place, drowned and buried by the sea.'

'Aye, said they so?' he sighed.

'Now that I have found you I will never leave you.'

'I maun return afore the break o' day.'

'I will come with you.'

'The place I bide is sma' and cauld,' said he.

'Not so small and cold I cannot warm you.'

'It is weit and it is daurk,' said he.

'Not so wet and dark I cannot kindle fire and light a lamp.'

'It is nae place for ye tae bide,' said he.

'Where your home is will be my home.'

'As you will,' said he and swept her up behind him on the great black horse.

On through the night they rode, the horse at a tireless gallop, past little sleeping townships, through glens and over mountain moorlands on through the sultry dark of the warm harvest night. And yet a shivering ran through the girl. She pulled her plaid about her shoulders and grasped the belt of her lover. Her hands brushed his clothes and recoiled for they were icy cold and wringing wet. A chill of fear ran into her.

'How is it, the night so warm and your clothes so cold and wet?'

Nothing he answered and spurred the black horse on through the dark. She pulled her plaid close about her and his coat flapped dank, cold and wet against her face.

'How is your coat so wet and icy cold?' she said.

And still he gave no answer, but on and on they rode until he reined the horse at last to a slow walk, guiding it between two great pillars. Before her rose the dark ruins of a church and all around her, gravestones.

'Come,' said he, 'here is our hame if ye will bide wi' me? It is sma' and weit and daurk but we will be again in company!' He slid from the horse.

She looked down, and in the leaden light she saw no face at all but white bone, a ghastly skull and hollow eyes, teeth that grinned, or did they girn at her in pain? She slithered from the horse and in a frenzy ran, jinking by the pale light of the moon past gravestones that seemed to rise in that eerie place to bar her way. Behind her close came clattering steps like bones rattling on the earth and a rasping of breath. For her life she ran. Long, skinny wisps of mist seemed to reach from graves to tangle her. Shadows leaped across her path. Always closer the rattling steps, the rasping breath. A strangling fear was in her throat when a hand clutched her tartan plaid and it tightened round her neck. The silver clasp of her brooch snapped as she fell to the ground and in cold terror turned to stone.

Shrill and sudden crowing cocks cried out on every side to greet the day and break the powers of night. In crimson fires morning flamed across the mountains in the east.

Wildly the girl looked round and saw no black horse nor spectral lover but the silent standing stones of graves and in those first red gleams of day she sank drowning from the world into unconsciousness.

There it was that two old men of the village discovered her, brought her to a cottage, laid her in the warmth of a box bed and covered her with a blanket of warm sheep's wool.

She lay in a delirium, feverous words tumbling from her lips, incoherent mutterings and mumblings of … a drowned man … a dancing man … a dead lover … dancing, dancing,

dancing ... a black stallion ... riding, riding, riding ... wet, wet, wet, his clothes cold and wet ... the brooch broken ... her plaid, her tartan plaid.

The villagers could make nothing of these wild words. Who was this stranger? No one knew her. No one could tell where she came from.

'The moon has taken the poor girl's wits.'

'She is surely mad.'

'But where is she from?'

'Who are her people?'

It was two days later that the old men who had found the girl were once more walking in the graveyard.

'I doubt her mind has gone,' said the one.

'Such broken talk, the words of a broken mind, but can there be nothing at all in her words? For how would she come here?'

'Look!' said the other, pointing suddenly to the ground. And there lay a plaid, a tartan plaid, and beside it a silver brooch with a broken clasp.

'There surely must be some truth in the girl's words. If we bring her the plaid maybe her mind will come back to her.'

The old man bent to lift it. But he could not for it lipped into the earth itself and was held fast. Try as they might they could not move it.

They reported this strange finding to the minister. He, pondering this uncanny affair, had spades brought and into the earth they dug to free the plaid, but always it stretched down till they came to a coffin. The end of the plaid was trapped under the lid.

Instructed by the minister, two men prised it open and there gripped in one white hand of bone was the plaid, but it was the face that fixed their gaze ... from the hollows that were his eyes little runnels ran – of tears or of decay, which they could not tell – drenching wet the clothes that clung to his bones. Gently the minister pulled the plaid from the clenched fingers.

They replaced the lid and covered the coffin once more with earth.

'Peace be with you restless spirit,' said the minister. 'In the name of Jesus Christ, may you find eternal rest.' Over the grave he made the sign of the cross.

Silently the little company returned to the village and made their way to the cottage where the girl lay, still restlessly mumbling in her delirium. They removed the blanket that covered her and over her laid her own tartan plaid. Almost immediately a peaceful sleep fell upon her. In the morning when she woke, the fever had gone and she was once more herself.

A few days later, when her strength returned, some of the villagers went with her to her own village far to the west. There she told her story and, taking heed at last of the words of the old cailleachs, 'Your tears will drown the spirit of the dead and keep him from his rest,' she wept no more.

Off to Kintail

Told by several Scottish Travellers, I first heard this story from the fine gentleman of the road, Willie McPhee. Each storyteller will put his or her own slant on the tale. Here is mine.

Now this story comes from dark times in the history of Scotland.

In a little glen in the Highlands, there lived a family: an old man, an old woman and their young son, Donald John McKinnon. For generations they had lived there. One day, word came to the glen that they were to be cleared from the land and that in their place there were to be sheep.

'Och, it is impossible,' they said, 'our fathers and forefathers have been here for generations. This cannot happen.'

But, in the course of a few weeks, the sheriff and his men came to the glen and they could see the trail of burning roofs as the band of men set fire to the thatches of the cottages and turned the people out and down to the sea. At last the sheriff's men came to the McKinnon house, and they were forced to leave and make their way down to the seashore. A hard winter fastened its grip on the Highlands and in that very year the old man and the old woman died, leaving Donald John McKinnon alone. Starvation stared him in the face.

Then one day he looked out to sea and he saw little fishing boats and thought, 'Now if I had a boat, I could survive.'

And so he spoke to the fishermen and, with a little bit of

their help, he found wood to make a beautiful boat which he fashioned with his big, strong hands. He began to fish.

Now the trouble was that he knew the ways of the land, but not of the sea. And one day as he was fishing he failed to notice a little wisp of wind becoming first of all a growl and then a howl, and the next moment the boat was pitching and tossing, turning and heaving in the sea. It cowped over, tossing Donald John McKinnon down, down, down into the cold depths of the sea. He saw his whole life pass before him and he thought indeed that this was his last moment.

When he came to, the sun was shining and as he looked around he thought, 'This must be paradise.' But it was not paradise. He was washed up on a little island just opposite the shore where he had kept his boat and where he had built a little house of stone.

He waded ashore and he thought, 'Now what a lucky man I am. But what about the boat?' And then along the shore he saw the boat. He came to it with a great cry of joy, but his joy turned to sadness when he realised that the boat was stoved in. There was a great hole in the stern. 'What am I going to do?' he thought. And then he looked at his big, strong hands and he said, 'If I made the boat, I can mend the boat.'

So he set off into the forest of Kintail looking for the exact right bit of wood to mend his boat. Some of the wood was twisted, some of it was overgrown. Some of it was covered in moss, some of it was rotted. He couldn't find the exact right bit that he needed.

What he didn't notice as he walked through the woods was that darkness was falling and from the sea there was coming a cold, white 'haar'. In a moment he could see nothing in front of him and he thought, 'I better not move. There could be creatures around. I could fall into a pit or into a marsh.'

Then in the distance he saw the glow of a little light and he thought, 'That could be a cottage, and if that's a cottage, that's shelter for the night, maybe even something to eat.'

So he made his way onwards and found that it was a cottage. As he approached, there was a little clearing and, in the half-light, he thought he could make out some barrels. 'Maybe it's just the stump of trees,' he thought. So he went up boldly to the door and knocked.

He heard an eerie and unnerving voice: 'That must be our guest. That must be Donald John McKinnon.'

And he thought, 'How would anyone know that I was coming?' He was just about to retreat when suddenly the door creaked open. Looking out at him were a pair of night-black eyes, long, crow-black, straggly hair and a long, bony finger beckoning him in, like a hook. Donald John McKinnon felt himself pulled into the cottage.

'Welcome, Donald John McKinnon,' said an old woman. 'Sit down.'

Now if this creature was ugly, the two others that sat at the table were equal in their ugliness. And so, as if propelled by the shoulders, he sat down, and together they said, 'Something to eat?' They pushed towards him what seemed like a bowl of slimy, pale grey porridge.

'Hmm ... no, thank you,' he said.

'Something to drink?' They pushed towards him something that looked like a bottle of whisky. He took this, lifted it to his lips and gulped it down.

'Oohhh!' He let out sigh. Had he been poisoned? The liquid was burning its way into his stomach.

All three women beckoned towards him with their long, bony fingers. 'Time for bed, Donald John McKinnon. We are going to help you in ways you would never expect.'

So he made his way to the little door that they had pointed to, opened it and went inside. He found himself in a room that was bare of everything – no bed, no table, no chairs. Only a hard packed earthen floor. As he stood there, bewildered by what had happened, he heard one of the voices say, 'Now, it is time!'

'Time for what?' he thought.

He put his eye to a little crack in the door and he saw one of these strange creatures approach what looked like a sea kist, an old sea chest. The mist must have cleared, for a slanted moon was shining upon the chest. One of the strange creatures dipped her hand in, pulled out a little tartan hat, placed it upon her head and then, 'Wheeeee!' she cried, 'off to London!' And she was gone, clean gone.

The second sister did the same – dipped her hand into the chest, pulled out a little tartan hat, placed it on her head. 'Wheeee! Off to London!' And with that she vanished. The third did likewise.

Donald John McKinnon carefully opened the door. There was the table. There was the slimy, cold porridge. There was the bottle of whisky. No sign of the three strange creatures.

Curious, he walked over and looked into the sea chest. There in one corner was a little tartan hat. 'Will I, or won't I?' he thought.

He lifted out the hat, and a voice in his head said, 'Be careful, Donald John McKinnon!' And then another voice said, 'Give it a tryyyyy!'

So he put the hat on his head and a voice said, 'Be careful Donald John McKinnon!' And the other voice said, 'Give it a tryyyyy!' That was the voice he listened to.

'Off to London!' he cried, and he found himself catapulted through the air, whirling, tumbling, tapsalteerie, head over heels through the blackness of the night. He landed with a clatter, looked around and thought, 'I should have listened to that other voice!'

It seemed that he'd arrived in a dungeon, stone walls all around. But, as he looked, he saw it was no dungeon, but rather a cellar with rows and rows of barrels disappearing down a passageway. Then, who should he see but the three strange sisters. One of them, a goblet in her hand, approached one of the barrels in which there was a little tap. She turned the tap, lifted the goblet to her lips and sipped. In that moment a most beautiful smile came across her face and she seemed transformed into a young, beautiful woman. 'Kintaaaiiillll!' she howled and was gone.

The second one did the same. She approached the barrel with a goblet, turned the tap, drank a sip and a smile crossed her face and she was transformed into a woman, young and beautiful. 'Kintaaaiiillll!' she cried and was gone. The third did the same, and Donald John McKinnon was left all alone.

'Where am I?' he thought. 'What's happening to me? Have I gone crazy? Was there something in that drink?'

Then his eye fell upon a goblet. He picked it up and a little voice in his head said, 'Be careful Donald John McKinnon!' But another voice said, 'Give it a tryyyyy!' So he took a gulp. Aaahhh! Oooooooohhhhhhh! How warm and beautiful it was. 'That's the best brandy I've ever tasted,' he thought. 'I think I'll have another.' So he did and then, 'Ho-ho,' he said, 'Ho-ho. I feel like singing a little song – lie-ti-ti, lie ti-ti.' He began to diddle a little song. 'Ho-ho, I feel like dancing.' And he began to do a little dance. Suddenly down upon his shoulder came a heavy hand.

'So, you're the one stealing the King's brandy!'

'Oh, no, no, no,' said Donald. 'It's the three sisters.'

'The only sisters is in your drunken head, Scotsman, and I wouldn't give much of a chance for it remaining too long on your body. The crime of stealing the King's brandy will not be looked upon very kindly.'

And indeed, Donald John McKinnon was taken to court. He was tried. He was sentenced to die by hanging.

'And to make an example,' said the judge, 'you'll get the tallest tree in England as the gallows.'

Fifty horsemen were sent to Sherwood. They came back with a great gallows tree. It was set up in the centre of London and Donald John McKinnon, the Scotsman, was brought out. As the rope was put around his neck, the hangman said,

'Well, have you any last request?'

'Well,' he said, 'I wonder if … um … if you would mind … er … if I wore my little tartan hat to die in?'

'Haw, haw, haw,' laughed the judge. 'Die in any hat you like, Scotsman. Have you any last word to say?'

Donald John McKinnon put the little hat on his head. 'Off to Kintaaaiiillll!' he cried.

He found himself whirling, tumbling, flying, hurtling, somersaulting through the air. He saw the whole of England flying past. He saw Scotland appearing, the beautiful hills of the Highlands. He came down soft, as soft as dandelion down and then there was a clatter beside him … and down fell the great gallows tree from England.

The rope was still around his neck. He took it off and found that he was back on his own little shoreline. And there beside him was his boat with the hole in it. He looked at the boat, he looked at the gallows tree. And he heard three voices in his head saying, 'We will help you in ways you would never expect!'

In that moment, he realised that this was the exact right piece of wood that he needed to mend his boat. With his big hands, he fashioned the wood and mended the boat. From that time on, the boat sailed as sure and as dainty as you like on the seas, whether the weather was rough or wild, in gale or storm or hurricane. It always sailed as if it was on the calmest of seas.

And Donald John McKinnon prospered and did well. His fishing was good, he married and had a family and he lived, as they say, happily ever after.

Yuki-Onna

This story I first heard in Japan from our guide, the storyteller Miki, when I was travelling and telling stories there with Mio Shudo in 2007. It is one of my favourite supernatural tales to tell, and a good one for a cold winter's night.

In a village of Musashi Province,
there once lived two woodcutters,
Mosaku and Minokichi.

Mosaku was an old man,
and Minokichi, his apprentice,
was a young man of eighteen.

Every day they went together to a forest,
about five miles from their village.
On the way there was a wide river,
which could only be crossed by a ferry.
Several times people had built a bridge,
but each time it was swept away
when the river flooded.

* * *

One bitterly cold evening
in the middle of winter,

Mosaku and Minokichi
were on their way home from the forest
when a great snowstorm overtook them.

When they reached the ferry,
with some difficulty,
they found that the boatman had already gone away
leaving his boat on the far side of the river.
It was certainly no day for swimming,
so Mosaku and Minokichi
decided to take shelter in the ferryman's hut.

It was a simple shelter
with no place to make a fire,
and with a single door
but no window.

* * *

Mosaku and Minokichi
were glad to have any shelter at all
on such a night.
They fastened the door tight,
and lay down to rest,
covering themselves with their straw raincoats.

At first, they did not feel so cold,
and they thought that the storm would soon pass.

The old man fell asleep almost immediately,
but Minokichi lay awake
listening to the howling wind
and the slashing of snow against the door.

YUKI-ONNA

The river was roaring
and the hut swayed
like a junk on the ocean.

It was a wild and terrible storm
and the air inside the hut
became colder and colder with every minute.

Minokichi shivered under his straw raincoat
and, at last, despite the cold
he too fell asleep.

* * *

He was wakened by a shower of snow on his face.
The storm was so fierce
that it had blown the door wide open.

And by the glow of the snow-light (yuki-akari)
he saw a woman in the room,
a woman all in white.

She was bending above Mosaku
and blowing her breath upon him.
It was like bright, white smoke.

Then, she turned to where Minokichi lay
and stooped over him.
He tried to cry out
but he was as if frozen,
and he found he could not make any sound.

The woman white as snow bent over him,
lower and lower,
until her face almost touched his.

He saw that she was very beautiful,
though her eyes put fear into him.

***

For a little while she gazed at him
and then she smiled and said,
'I intended to do with you as with the old man,
but you are so young.
I feel pity for you.
You are a pretty boy, Minokichi
and I will not harm or hurt you now.
But –
if ever you tell anyone,
even your own mother,
what you have seen this night …
I will kill you!
Remember what I say. Remember!'

With these words she turned from him
and passed through the doorway.

***

Minokichi found that he could now move:
he sprang up,
looked out.
But the woman was nowhere to be seen.

The snow was driving furiously into the hut,
so Minokichi closed the door,
securing it with spars of wood.

Had the wind blown the door open?
Had he been dreaming?

Had he mistaken the snow-light in the door
for a woman?

He called over to Mosaku,
and was frightened to have no answer.
In the dark of the hut
he reached out his hand and touched Mosaku's face –
and found it was ice!
Mosaku was stark and dead.

***

By dawn the storm was past.
When the ferryman returned to his hut,
a little after dawn,
he found Minokichi unconscious,
lying beside the dead body of Mosaku.

Minokichi was looked after,
but he was a long time ill,
with recurring memories of that terrible night.
He had been greatly frightened by the old man's death,
but he said nothing of the vision of the woman in white.

At last he was well enough to return to work, alone,
and his old mother helped him
to sell the bundles of wood that he gathered in the forest.

***

One evening,
in the winter of the following year,
on his way home from the forest,
Minokichi overtook a girl travelling by the same road.

She was tall and slim
and of great beauty.
She answered Minokichi's greeting
with a voice sweet on the ear,
the voice of a songbird.

They talked as they walked on along the road,
and the girl told Minokichi
that her name was O-Yuki.
She had lately lost both her parents
and was travelling to Yedo to visit relatives there
who might be able to help her find work as a servant.

Minokichi soon felt charmed by this strange girl.
The more he looked at her,
and talked with her,
the more he liked her.
He asked if she was betrothed.
She laughed and said she was free.
Was he married or pledged?

He told her that he lived with his widowed mother,
and the question of
'an honourable daughter-in-law'
had not yet been raised.
He was still very young.

* * *

After this exchange
they walked for a while in silence but,
as the saying goes,
'When the wish is there,
the eyes can say as much as the mouth.'

By the time they reached the village,
they had become very much pleased with each other.
Minokichi asked O-Yuki to rest a while at his house.
His mother made her welcome
and prepared a warm meal for her.
O-Yuki behaved so nicely
that Minokichi's mother took a sudden fancy to her,
and persuaded her to delay her journey to Yedo.

And the natural end of the matter
was that O-Yuki never went to Yedo at all –
she remained in the house
and became the 'honourable daughter-in-law'.

* * *

O-Yuki proved a fine daughter-in-law.
When, in five years,
Minokichi's mother died,
her last words were in praise of her fine daughter-in-law.
O-Yuki bore ten children, boys and girls,
all of them handsome,
and very fair of skin.

The country folk thought O-Yuki wonderful,
yet so different in nature from themselves.
Most peasant women age early,
but she stayed as fresh and young and fair
as the first day she came to the village.

* * *

One evening,
after the children were asleep,
O-Yuki sat sewing by the light of a paper lantern.

Minokichi was watching her.

'When I see you sitting there
with the lantern light on your face
it makes me think of a strange thing that happened to me
when I was eighteen.
It was the only other time
that I've seen anyone as beautiful as you …
indeed she looked very like you.'

O-Yuki did not lift her eyes from her sewing:

'Tell me about her. Where did you see her?'

Minokichi told her of that terrible night
in the ferryman's hut,
about the woman in white
who had stooped over him,
smiling,
whispering,
and about the silent death of old Mosaku.

He said,
'Asleep or awake
it was the only time that I saw
a being as beautiful as you!
But she was no human being –
I was afraid of her, very afraid!
So white she was.
And I've never been sure
whether it was a dream I saw,
or the woman of the snow.'

* * *

O-Yuki put down her sewing,
arose and bowed over Minokichi,
lower and lower.
And then she shrieked:
'It was I – I – I, Yuki, it was I!
And I told you then that I would kill you
if ever you spoke one word about that night.

But for the children asleep there,
I would kill you this moment.
For now, you had better take very good care of them,
for if they have any reason to complain of you,
I will treat you as you deserve.'

***

Even as she screamed,
her voice grew thin,
like a far crying in the wind.
And then she faded into a bright, white mist
that spiralled to the roof beams
and shimmered away through the smoke hole.
O-Yuki was never seen again.

Gregor Armstrong

This suspenseful, eerie tale I adapted from a traditional Borders tale that Duncan Williamson and I heard from a strange old man in a pub in Selkirk.

I was with my good friend, storyteller Duncan Williamson, in Selkirk. It was the middle of winter, the thirteenth of December, and we'd been telling stories in a school all day; I was quite tired. We were walking along and we came by a little churchyard on a hill. It was just beginning to get a little dark. Then, from the graveyard we heard a high-pitched, eerie screech.

I said to Duncan, 'What's that?'

'It's a GHOST!!' he replied. He was always up for nonsense.

'That's not a ghost. It's more like a cat or the wind,' I said.

'There's no wind today, David,' he said. 'It's a ghost.'

We decided to have a half pint before we went home. There was a little pub. I forget what it was called; it was maybe called the Travellers' Rest. It was a beautiful little pub, all wood, a real fire in the corner and an old man sitting there.

'Do you believe in ghosts?' Duncan asked me.

'Well,' I said, 'my mum said she had once seen the ghost of my brother after he'd been killed in the war.'

At that moment, this old man came over to us and said, 'I hear you two talking about ghosts. Would you mind if I join you?'

'Not at all,' we said.

'I'll tell you a story,' he said. 'I'll tell you a story about a man from this town.'

And this is the story he told us:

There was a man called Gregor Armstrong. He was a thin, weaselly kind of man, with thin bony fingers. He loved one thing in the world, only one thing – money. He was a cobbler; he made shoes morning till night, Monday, Tuesday, Wednesday, Thursday, Friday, Saturday and Sunday.

He had married a beautiful Highland lady and nobody knew why she had married Gregor. He was a very, very mean man, a grasping man, a greedy man. His wife would say to him, 'Gregor, could you give me a little money to feed the children?'

'I gave you money on Tuesday!'

'But Gregor, that's nearly a week ago. The children are hungry and look at the little one – you're a shoemaker, but he's completely through his shoes. His feet will be bleeding in no time.'

'Make that last,' and out of his purse he pulled a few coins.

One day he was walking down the road and he met the minister. 'Mr Armstrong, we haven't seen you in church for some time. When will you be coming back?'

'When I've got enough money.'

'That might be too late,' said the minister.

The strange thing was that that night Gregor Armstrong went to his bed early and awoke at four o'clock in the morning when the big grandfather clock went boom, boom, boom. Up jumped Gregor and put on the little, red woollen hat that he always wore and went down to his workroom in the shop and started to make his shoes.

As he did, suddenly he felt a strange, eerie chill creeping through his body and he felt as if behind him there was a dark shadow. Looking round, sideways, he could see a tall, dark figure. Turning his head, he saw a tall, tall man wearing a long, black coat and a big, old black hat, and when he looked up he saw the face was paper thin, the eyes glittering. He had long, thin hands and on his feet, no shoes; they were like a skeleton's feet, covered with a thin layer of skin. Then the figure spoke in a strange, hoarse voice as if it was unused to human speech. It said but one word, 'Shoes.'

The figure then stretched out a hand and Gregor thought it was going for his throat. But no, it reached up to a shelf where Gregor kept his most beautiful shoes, a pair of beautiful shoes with silver buckles; nobody ever knew where he got them. The figure took down these shoes, then bending down in a creaky way, slipped them on to his feet, straightened himself slowly and said one word, 'Perfect.'

Gregor watched as the figure stretched his hand under his cloak and pulled out an old leather purse with a pearl button. He opened the purse and then Gregor's eyes danced, for in his hand he held one big, fat, gold coin. But Gregor's eyes were arrested by the purse, for in it he could see something wriggling and squirming. The figure dropped the coin on the counter. Gregor gave a start, and without another word the figure moved towards the door and click, click, he disappeared. Now Gregor knew the door was locked, so he ran across. It was still locked, bolted above, bolted in the middle, bolted below. Gregor was bewildered. He thought he must have dreamed it. He sat down, but there on the counter was the big, fat, gold coin. He grasped it, put it in a drawer, looked at the shelf – the shoes were gone.

Gregor was curious, but above all Gregor was greedy. He went to the door, unbolted it, unlocked it and followed the figure through the morning dark mist of that December day, click, click, click, click up a narrow street, down a little vennel, along by an old wall, past the two great pillars. He disappeared into the churchyard and Gregor hid behind a tombstone. Just at that moment, the sun rose in a long beam and Gregor's courage got up. He saw the figure leaping into an open grave. He ran across but when he got there, there was nothing; it was grown over as if it had never been in any way disturbed.

Gregor was obsessed, obsessed by his shoes with the silver buckles. He would get them back. So he did a very strange thing. He knocked on the doors of some other tradesmen. They hadn't seen him for years. He invited them back to his house, told them the story.

'Gregor,' they said, 'things like that don't happen. People don't walk through doors that are bolted.'

Gregor said, 'It happened. My beautiful shoes are gone.'

Of course they didn't believe him. They said, 'Gregor, the trouble with you is you've been working too hard. What you need, to be quite frank, is a doctor.'

'There's nothing wrong with me! Nothing wrong with my mind! It's as clear as your own minds. This is exactly what happened and I can show you the place.'

So one of them said, 'We'll humour him, we'll get a bottle of whisky,' and so it was they got a bottle of whisky, some picks and shovels and went along to the graveyard.

'Well, Gregor,' said one of them, 'where did your fine man jump into the grave?'

'Here,' said Gregor, and he showed them the place.

One of them laughed, because the gravestone, though covered with moss, had on it the name 'Armstrong'.

'It's got your name on it, Gregor.'

He said, 'Dig!' and they dug down and down and down.

One of them said, 'Do you want us to dig to Australia, Gregor?' At that moment, the spade hit the wood of a coffin.

'Dig it out,' said Gregor.

So they dug around it, brought the coffin up and prised open the lid. There, true to Gregor's words, was a man in black, and on his feet were the shoes with the silver buckles.

'These are my shoes,' said Gregor. 'I'm taking these shoes.' And with that he tore them off.

'Gregor, this is unholy business, this is eerie work,' said the others. 'We want nothing more to do with this.'

'You took it out. Put it back in!' So they did, quick as they could, covered it with the earth, stamped it over. They went home, not one speaking to the other.

When Gregor got home, he was delighted. He rubbed his hands. He had the shoes with the silver buckles and he had one big, fat, gold coin. All was well.

Now you might think that Gregor would have been happy with that. You might think that he would have been content, but no, no, not Gregor. Once again, when four o'clock in the morning struck, up got Gregor, put on his little, red, woollen hat and down he went.

And his wife heard a very strange thing – Gregor Armstrong singing! 'He must have come by some money, something he's not told me about,' she thought. But at that moment, the singing changed into a wild, strangled howl. Through the house came the screaming, howling like an animal. The door burst open, the little ones came in, 'Mummy! Mummy! Mummy! Daddy's screaming, Daddy's howling ...'

'Shhhh,' she said. And she put them on the bed and said, 'Wait you here, wait you here.'

She went down the stairs, opened the door, looked into the workshop. Everything was undisturbed except that the door was open. No sign of Gregor. She went outside, she went to the neighbours, she knocked on the door.

The neighbour said, 'What is it? What is it, Mrs Armstrong?'

'Will you run in and look after the bairnies?' she said. 'I must find my husband.'

And she went through the town, she looked up and down, high and low until at last she was exhausted. She went to the door of the minister.

'Mrs Armstrong,' he said, 'you look as though you've seen a ghost.'

'Oh, don't say that,' she said. 'Gregor has disappeared. I don't know where he's gone.'

'Well, come in and have a cup of tea.'

There was a church elder with the minister.

'Oh, minister,' said Gregor's wife, 'I heard a sound this morning that I've never heard the like of, my husband howling as if devils were tearing him apart.'

'Where is he now?' asked the minister.

'I don't know,' she said.

'You know, I saw Gregor Armstrong yesterday with one or two of our parishioners. They were in the graveyard with picks and shovels,' said the elder.

'Indeed!' said the minister. 'Do you know these men?'

They found those men, who confessed that they had been in the graveyard.

'Then back we'll go,' said the minister. 'Bring your picks and shovels.'

Back they trooped, an unhappy little crowd of men. They came to the graveyard and the minister said, 'Where did you dig?'

'It was here, sir.'

'Here?' asked the minister. 'This hasn't been dug in years, for centuries.'

It was all grown over as it had always been.

But one of them said, 'Look, sir.' And they looked at the gravestone which yesterday had been encrusted with moss and now had the name 'Armstrong' glinting in the sun as if it had been carved in diamonds.

'This is where it was, sir.'

'Well, dig,' said the minister.

They dug and they dug and they dug, and at length they came to the coffin.

'Take it out,' said the minister.

They took it out, fearful and reluctant, and once more they prised off the lid. And there, lying in the grave, was the man in black. But now there was a difference. The men said, 'Look, sir.' And on his feet were the two shoes with the silver buckles. But one arm was folded across his chest and the other was twisted to the side. His eyes had a kind of glint. There was a grin, you might say, on his face and his right arm was lifted and in that hand, tightly clenched, was Gregor Armstrong's knitted, red woollen hat.

And that was the last that was ever heard or seen or known of Gregor Armstrong.

The old man in the bar looked at us.

'That was my great, great, great grandfather, and we still have that hat in the house. Would you like to come and see it?'

'Hmm, no, no, it's alright,' I said.

He looked at Duncan. 'Would you like to see the little, red hat?'

There was something eerie about this old man. Duncan said, 'No, no, it's alright, we have to get back to Edinburgh.'

And so we got into the car and started off for Edinburgh. But then Duncan turned and said, 'David, I'm really sorry, but I've left my hat in the pub.'

So I turned round and we drove back to the pub.

We got back there and I said, 'Excuse me, my friend's left his hat.'

'Aye,' said the barman. 'It's over yonder on the table.'

I said, 'What happened to our friend, the old man?'

'What old man are you talking about?' said the barman.

I said, 'The old man who was sitting beside us, telling us a story.'

'What old man?'

'The old man who was sitting at the fire. He came over and was talking to us, telling us a story.'

'There's been no old man in here tonight. There's been just your two selves. Business is bad enough. I would have noticed any other customer.'

'But there was an old man ...'

'Don't be arguing with me. If you've been drinking, this is not the place for you! This is not a pub for argument.'

So we left.

Duncan said, 'What do you make of that?'

I said, 'What do you make of the old man?'

Duncan said, 'I dunno. What do you make of his story?'

'I don't know,' I said.

And to this day, the whole thing has remained a mystery.

The Minister and the Skull

A Traveller tale from Willie MacPhee.

Long since, but not so long since these times and events are remembered in the townships of a Scottish Highland glen, there lived an old minister.

In his philamore, his great tartan plaid, he had walked the glens and straths of his widespread parish. It was ever his joy and custom to rise before the sun had lifted the mist from the hills or the dew from the grass and he would visit his flock near and far, often in the farthest glens.

He was their good shepherd, much loved, and always a welcome awaited him: bannocks, tea and, as night drew on, usquabae, the hospitality of the news, the stories and the song.

But the years had come on him. One winter's day, travelling homewards late in the glen, he was caught in a wild blizzard. He was found, holding his crummock, frozen white in the snow, gazing as if to the mountain tops.

'Just like an angel, just like an angel,' said the old bodachs and cailleachs of the glens.

In his place came a young scholar from the Lowlands educated at New College Edinburgh, a stranger to the Highland ways.

Long and fiery and fierce were his sermons: sin, judgement, death, punishment, the pains of hell. The grip of Satan was his theme, damned to an eternity of suffering those who blasphemed God's holy Sabbath, tenfold the agony of those who broke the commandments. Long into the night he pored over the words of the Old Testament, his favourite book, Job and his tomes of theology.

One day this earnest young man was walking at the gloaming hour, the hour of half-light, through the graveyard, contemplating death and judgement and searching for inspiration for the next day's sermon. He came beyond the graveyard, through bush and fern, in the shade of an ancient yew tree, to a small and older graveyard, and in it to an old tomb, a mausoleum. And lying there now, glinting in the moonlight, a skull, a human skull. This skull had beautiful teeth, perfect beautiful teeth.

The young minister, who himself had fine teeth of which he was rather proud, was gazing at this skull, admiring the teeth, when the skull spoke: 'I see you like my teeth,' it said. 'You're admiring my teeth.'

The young minister was astounded. 'Well, that's true,' he said, 'yes.'

'Ye've got fine teeth yourself,' said the skull. 'And what brings ye here? Ye're the first visitor I've seen for many a long weary year, I can tell ye.'

Soon the minister and the skull were deep in conversation, in talk of the Bible, of theology, of the minister's favourite book, Job.

At last the minister said, 'I've not had such a lively conversation for years. There's no one around here can talk about these things. It's been a pleasure. Could we meet again?'

'Well,' said the skull, 'I could visit you. I could do with a wee bit of an airing.'

The minister was overjoyed. 'Come at three o'clock tomorrow to the manse,' said he.

'I know the place. I'll be there,' said the skull. 'Three o'clock.'

The young minister was delighted. Here was someone he could talk to. Now he had found a friend, someone instructed in his beloved theology. He told his old housekeeper he was expecting a visitor and next day he could hardly contain himself for excitement.

Scones and tea and a chair were ready. The grandfather clock struck three.

No skull appeared.

A few minutes past three and the minister called to the housekeeper.

'Do you see anything coming up the path …?'

'Well, sir,' she said, 'I see something like a turnip or cabbage, something round rolling along the road.'

'Open the door,' said he.

And in a few minutes in rolled the skull.

'Sorry I'm a bit late,' said the skull, 'I lost track of time.'

'Not at all,' said the minister. 'Make yourself comfortable … a bannock and cheese. Will you join me?'

'To tell you the truth,' said the skull, 'I don't have the stomach for it.'

And once again the conversation was long and deep and theological.

Time flew by and, as dark gathered, the skull said, 'Well, I must be rolling along now. Shall we meet again?'

'With pleasure,' said the minister.

'Well,' said the skull, 'you can come to the place where I used to bide, long, long since. Make your way through the old graveyard and beyond that ye'll find a path, a sheep track deep in the woods. Come by horseback for it's a fair step ye'll need to come. And on the way deep into the woods you'll come to a clearing and a quarry there, by a three hundred-year-old tree. Then you'll come to a big mansion house and you'll come to a farmhouse. Now whatever ye see on the way, say nothing, do nothing, only look. For you will see strange sights, eerie sights, uncanny sights.'

So they arranged the day, and the minister saddled his horse and set off bright and early.

True to the word of his friend the skull, he found through the old graveyard the path leading into the wood, and travelling on, he came to the clearing and the quarry. And there in the quarry, stripped to the waist, two men. They were shovelling gravel out of a pit, but always as they shovelled the gravel fell back, spadeful after spadeful. They were sweating and groaning and straining, and their faces contorted in pain.

The minister gazed at them in wonder. He looked but said nothing.

And on he rode through a glen and came by and by to a great mansion house. He heard a shrieking and screeching and screaming. Outside the house, bound to a tree, was an old woman, and he saw a young woman with a birch branch in her hand battering, beating, lashing, hammering into this old woman who was howling, yowling, shrieking, pleading for mercy.

The minister was horrified but he said nothing. He looked and rode on.

On he rode until he came to a farmhouse. And there at the open door a stout woman like a farmer's wife, her eyes wide with terror and her mouth wide open. From her mouth rats and mice came scuttling, running in and out.

Amazed, the minister watched. He said and did nothing and rode on.

At last he came to an old stone manse, ivy-covered and gloomy. As he tethered his horse, he heard the voice of his friend the skull.

'Come in, come in. Welcome.'

And in he came. Tea, scones and bannocks and a bottle of whisky were laid out and two armchairs. The skull settled in one.

'Help yourself,' he said. 'I'll not be needing anything.'

But the minister was shaken, pale and without an appetite.

'Ye're looking a thing pale and wabbit,' said the skull. 'Maybe a wee dram would help.'

For once the minister took a stiff dram.

'I know what it is,' said the skull. 'It's the sights ye met on the way.'

'It is,' said the minister, 'it is.'

'Well,' said the skull, 'these sights were the very parables you've preached,' said he. 'These two men digging in the quarry were brothers, they broke the Lord's Day, the Holy Sabbath, working on the Sunday, breaking the command of God and so now their punishment is labour in vain.

That woman you saw bound to a tree was a woman of great wealth and she hired a poor peasant serving girl. She worked her, she whipped her, she starved her to death. And now she has the whipping and beating she gave that girl.

A poor tinker woman with a hungry bairn came to the door of that stout farmer's wife you saw, the rats and mice scuttling and running in and out of her mouth. She was begging a sup of milk. The farmer's wife had a keg she knew a rat had drowned in and she gave the woman milk from that vat for the bairn and poisoned the little one. And what you saw was her tenfold punishment.'

'Oh, dear God,' said the minister … and fell silent.

And so they sat and talked like old friends till the sun grew low. The skull said, 'And how long, old friend, do you think we have been sitting here?'

'It seems no time, but it may be three hours,' said the minister.

'So it seems,' said the skull. 'Time has a strange way. Now heed my words – take with you your sackcloth. Before you alight from the saddle, put it on the ground for your feet. Ride on and you will see strange sights. Heed them not and when you come into a town you will see an old woman throwing water over steps. Ask if she heard tell of a minister of long ago.'

And so, taking the sackcloth, the minister took leave of his friend, mounted his horse and rode on. And strange to his eyes and his ears was that journey. For across the sky came a great roaring, like a giant bird of metal with flashing lights. The road was hard and smooth and flat, and thundering past on rails of iron came monstrous wagons full of people. Great buildings rose around him and crowds of boys laughed and shouted and pointed at this lone man on a horse, dressed in black like a ghost from another age.

Then he saw an old woman, in an old part of the town, washing steps, throwing over them a bucket of water.

'Can you tell me,' he said, 'have you ever heard of a minister from these parts who disappeared?'

'Auld wives' tale, sir,' said she. 'My granny told me there was a tale, oh, a hundred or more years ago,' she said. 'She said there was a minister – a crazy man who was supposed to have spoken with a skull, a dead man's skull. But I'm sure there was no such man. Auld tales.'

'I was just that man,' said the minister. 'I am that man.'

'You're mad, sir – tae spread such things.'

With that, the minister leaped from the horse in fury, forgetting the cloth of sack. Dust filled the air. And a skull rolled down to the old church hall.

Today, if you should find that ancient graveyard, you will see an old tomb, a mausoleum. And side by side, two shiny skulls, each with perfect, sparkling teeth.

The Holy Horse

My friend Dolina McLennan, a fine Gaelic singer, storyteller and actor from the Hebridean island of Lewis, told me this tale. The islands are well known for their strict form of Presbyterian Christianity, an atmosphere in which Doli grew up. There are those who baulk at the repression; this story is an expression of that rebellious spirit.

This is the story of a minister – it is a story of his disaster. He was a minister in the Hebrides, the islands to the west of Scotland. He was the minister on the island of Lewis and right on the most northerly point, the Butt of Lewis.

In that place, ministers are chosen for the length of their faces and the gloominess of their voices. This one had a long face. He was a long man, always in black, a long, thin man with long, thin legs, long, thin arms and long, thin fingers.

His voice was dark with gloom. His sermons were long, but not thin. They were thick with threats of the fires of hell to come to consume poor mortal sinners.

Well, he was very sad, this minister, sad because his horse had died and his horse was a most important creature. On his horse he would ride to every part of his far-flung parish and, greeting a wayward member of his congregation, admonish, 'I didn't see you in church on Sunday. Why not?' And he would glower with his long, ministerial face at the quaking sinner.

Or he would ride to a cottage at the far end of the isle and growl like gathering of thunder, 'I saw you late, late on Saturday night walking from the hotel and your legs were wobbly. You know, don't you, that drink is the Devil's invitation to perpetual suffering in hell?'

To others he would growl, 'You have not been on your knees enough in prayers to the Lord. Your soul is growing flabby with the weight of the flesh.'

So when his horse died it was a matter of great importance to the minister. How could he keep his widespread flock under the chastising rod of the Lord, of which he was the chosen shepherd?

Now there were some bad pieces of news for the minister. One was that the only person on the island who sold horses was that godless, tight-fisted Angus. Angus kept very good horses but Angus always wanted more than a good price. Angus knew the value of a penny. And Angus never darkened the door of a church. Angus was an avowed atheist. Now that was bad news for the minister, but there was worse. You know how news will travel in a small community, and on an island – swift as light. That morning the minister had met the pier master in the village street.

'Oh, good morning minister,' said he, 'there's a parcel waiting for you down at the pier.'

'Good, good, good,' said the minister, 'that will be my theological books.'

'Well, you'd better hurry to collect them,' said the harbour master, 'because one of them is leaking.'

So Angus, of course, was already in possession of this little piece of useful information when he saw the minister later that very morning walking over the island.

'Good mo-o-orning, Angus!' said the minister in his long, gloomy voice, as gloomy as his long face.

'Good morning, minister!' said Angus. 'I see you are walking this morning.'

'Yes, Angus,' said the minister, 'my horse has died.'
'Oh,' said Angus, 'well, you'll be needing a new horse.'
'Yes, Angus, this is why I came to see you.'
'Och, minister, I have the very horse for you.'
'I'd thought you'd say so, Angus.'
'Och no, minister, this is a holy horse.'
'There's no such thing as a holy horse, Angus.'
'Oh yes, minister, I wouldn't even be surprised if it was a Presbyterian like yourself. Hey-heh!'
'Angus, I don't consider that a matter of comedy.'
'Minister, I assure you, this is a religious horse – it is the very horse for you.'
'There's no use overstating its qualifications, Angus!'
'I'll just show you, minister!' and he brought out the most beautiful horse in the world.

It was a fine, white horse, long flowing mane, flowing tail, white, beautiful in every point. The minister was impressed. It could have been a horse that had walked through the gates of paradise – indeed, it was a heavenly appearance of a horse.

'Yes, Angus, it's a good-looking creature. But what would make you say it is a holy horse?'

'Well,' said Angus, 'let's just go in and discuss a price, shall we? We could talk about it over a wee dram.'

'I don't drink, Angus,' said the minister.

'Och no,' said Angus, 'I forgot. You spend your time reading your theological books.'

'What makes you say it is a holy horse, Angus?'

'Well, minister, this horse will only walk if you mount her, take the reins, lean forward, give her a little clap and say bless you!'

'And likewise, minister, to get her to trot, a little clap and bless you! And the same to canter and to gallop the same.'

'Yes, yes, yes, very well Angus. And how much do you want for this creature?'

'Ahem, two hundred and fifty pounds?'

'That's not a religious price, Angus. One hundred and fifty!'

'Two hundred and twenty-five?'

'Two hundred?'

'Done!'

The minister handed over the two hundred pounds. 'Now Angus, if you're telling me a lie you will roast in hell!'

'Oh, I might if I believed in that place, minister. He-he-he,' and he laughed his little goat-like laugh.

So the minister mounted the horse.

'Minister?' said Angus.

'Ye-e-es, Angus?'

'Minister, you'll want to know how to get the creature to stop.'

'Well, Angus, how do you get the creature to stop?'

'I told you she was a holy horse. In order to get her to stop you just say amen!'

'Yes, yes, yes, Angus!' But he didn't believe Angus. He pulled the reins and dug in his heels. The horse didn't move. Reluctantly, he gave the horse a muttered bless you, and to his amazement, clack-clack, clack-clack, clack-clack, clack-clack.

'Angus was speaking the truth,' he said to himself, 'oh, Angus was speaking the truth.'

The horse began to walk a nice, gentle walk, clip-clop, clip-clop, clip-clop. 'I wonder if she will trot? Bless you!' he said and gave her a little clap. And off she went, clickety-click, clickety-click, clickety-click, down the road in a lovely, little trot.

He was posting along. 'A beautiful day,' he said. 'I wonder if she will canter. Bless you,' said he. Off she went in a golden canter. And there they were going over bens and glens and mountain moorlands, past little clachan villages.

'Och, good morning, Morag,' he said. 'Be sure I see you in church on Sunday!' And the minister was riding through the island, the sweetest of mornings.

'Oh, good morning, Donald. I'll be visiting you on Saturday evening. Be sure you are at home!' and on he rode.

And he thought, 'I'll see if she'll gallop.' He gave her a great crack and a bless you and off she went – like the wind! Wildly galloping across the island, the minister was in a state of feverish exhilaration. He was sweating, the horse was sweating. It was really a state of thrilling ecstasy the minister was in as he rode wild and free over the island. Suddenly he thought, 'We're nearing the end of the island.'

And if you've been in Lewis, you'll know that at the north of the island, at the Butt of Lewis, there is a cliff that falls sheer into the sea about a hundred metres. And so the minister knew he'd have to stop the horse. But in the wild gallop his mind went blank ... he couldn't remember the word. And so they were flying towards the edge of the island, towards the cliff, towards the sea. Being a holy man, however, he began to say the Lord's Prayer. So at the full gallop he was saying, 'Our Father, which art in heaven, hallowed-be-thy-name-thy-kingdom-come-thy-will-be-done-on-earth-as-it-is-in-Heaven-give-us-this-da-de-da-dit – AMEN!'

And the horse skidded to a halt, so-o-o-o close to the edge of the cliff that its two feet were on the edge and its head was actually sticking over the cliff looking down at the raging sea.

The minister was so relieved he leaned forward, clapped the beautiful horse and sighed, 'Bless you!'

Archie's Besom

This tale I heard Duncan Williamson tell with great relish. The sentiments clearly appealed to him and the setting was home ground to Duncan, as was the craft of making heather besoms. This was a Gaelic story that Duncan had learned from his friend, Neil MacCallum.

Many years ago there lived two old brothers who were skilled drystane dyke builders. Archie, the youngest was, folk would have said, not the smartest card in the pack, but was good-natured, strong and a fine worker. Donald was the boss and it was, 'Archie do this, do that, fetch the eggs, milk the cow, sweep the floor.' It was Archie's task to lift the stones for the dyke and pass them to his brother who was a skilled dyker.

One day the brothers were building a dyke for a farmer when along the road came a Travelling man, a tinker, a broom-maker who made beautiful heather besoms much in demand by country folk. Where Archie and Donald were working grew fine heather bushes.

The Traveller-tinker stopped to pass the time of day and said to Donald, 'Would ye mind if I took some of this heather to mak ma besoms?'

'Mind?' said Donald, 'take as much as you like, it's no use to us.'

So the tinker broom-maker began to pull, cut and gather bundles of heather.

Archie was fascinated and said to the tinker, 'But what do you do with that heather to make a besom?'

'Och, I gather it tae a bunch, tie it roond the handle, trim the taps o' the heather and I've got a broom.'

'You've got a broom?'

'Aye. I've got a broom tae sell.'

'What would you get for the broom?'

'I'd get a shilling, maybe two shillings.'

'How long would you take to make it?'

'Maybe twenty minutes. I'd mak three or fower in an 'oor.'

'You'd make eight shillings! And here I am working the whole day for a shilling!'

'Weel,' said the broom-maker, 'I'll bid ye baith guid day an' I'm on ma way.'

'Archie' said Donald, 'you've been blethering long enough. Pass me that stone.'

'No,' said Archie. 'No!'

'What do you mean, no?'

'That's me finished with carting stones.'

'Archie, pass me that stone at your feet!'

'No, I've lifted the last stone. I'm going into business.'

Donald laughed. 'And what kind of business are you going into Archie?'

'I'm going to be a broom-maker to make more in a day than you pay me in a week. I'm finished!'

'Archie,' said Donald, 'these tinker-men are skilled.'

'He told me how to do it. I'm off to work.' Off he went, whistling and gathering heather on the way.

Back in their wee croft, he went into the barn, cut one of his brother's good byre brushes. And Archie gathered a big bunch of heather round the handle, tied it with binder twine and trimmed the heather with shears: and he had a brush, a big, sprawling, bushy brush. Proudly he showed it to Donald.

'Nobody, nobody's going to buy a thing like that Archie. Nobody. You're not going to shame us with trying to sell that ugly thing, and me an elder of the kirk!'

But next morning Archie was off down the road into the village with his besom. Proudly, he knocked on a cottage door. 'I'm selling besoms, only two shillings,' and he held up his big, bushy heather broom.

As soon as the woman set her eyes on it, she said, 'No, no, sorry. I'm not needing that kind of broom.'

At every house it was the same; one look was enough. As he came out of the village, there was one cottage set back on a hill. By now he was disheartened. Archie was kind of ashamed of his broom and hid it behind his back.

To the door came Maggie, known to the villagers as 'Fat Maggie'. She had black hair, dark eyes and was as broad as she was high. 'What can I do for you?' said she, glowering at Archie.

He slowly drew the besom from behind his back.

Maggie's dark eyes danced. For what Archie didn't know was that 'Fat Maggie' was a witch. That night there was to be a gathering of witches in the birch woods of Kintail and Maggie had no transportation, no broom strong enough for her to fly on. Maggie was in love with Archie's besom!

'It is a shilling,' said Archie.

'A shilling, a shilling!' said Maggie. 'No, for a beautiful broom like that, five shillings.' Into Archie's hand she put five silver shillings. Her eyes glinted. 'Every time you spend one of these, my good man, another will take its place.'

She closed the door and put her legs astride the broom. Up, up, up sailed she and floated round the room and out of the door. 'Ha, ha,' she cackled. 'Up and away. You're in for a surprise the nicht, ye hags!'

Meantime in the birch wood of Kintail, the coven of witches had gathered as clouds passed over the full moon. They were laughing, chortling, crowing.

'Ha, Fat Maggie can't come! Fat Maggie can't find a broomstick strong enough to carry her!' They were prancing and dancing with glee! Beside them were their besoms. 'Ha,' they chorused, 'no transportation. Fat Maggie has no transportation!'

At that moment the clouds cleared and a dark shadow crossed the face of the moon. Maggie, on Archie's besom. Down she floated and landed in their midst. 'So!' she gloated, 'Maggie, cannae get a broom for carrying her! Nae Maggie the nicht. Weel, Maggie's here. Maggie flew here an' yous willnae flee hame!'

With that she gathered the witches' besoms in her arms and threw them into the wind, where they were blown into the branches of the birch trees of Kintail. There they stuck. There you can see them to this day. Far and wide you will see them, like crow's nests, stuck in the birch trees all over Scotland.

Cackling, Maggie flew home.

Girning and groaning, the witches walked.

Auld Cruvie

This I heard from the eloquent Aberdeenshire Traveller storyteller, Stanley Robertson. Stanley had a great gift for eerie and moody stories. I always remember one morning in my kitchen when two electricians were doing work, and asked what we were up to. I said, 'My friend Stanley is about to tell a story. Come and listen.' Stanley was at his eerie best and told the ghostly story of the old woman who lived alone, when she had a strange visitor. At the conclusion of this story, Stanley let out a wild howl with the line, 'I've come to get you!' Two electricians leapt as if electrocuted, as did the rest of us. Stanley had his desired effect. As well as being a master of the supernatural, Stanley had a deeply compassionate nature which the story of Auld Cruvie epitomises.

Jack lived with his mother in a wee cottage.
They were poor but Jack, a kind and honest lad,
worked for his master
the Laird of the Black Airts,
cruel as he was mean.

From morning till dusk,
Jack looked after the laird's sheep on the hill.

Poorly paid as Jack was,
he loved his work.

He loved the sheep, the land, the river that ran by
and would watch the salmon's silver leap.
He knew and loved the song of every bird,
could tell when each joined the orchestra of the dawn,
loved the little creatures of the land and forest.
He was content.
Especially Jack loved the trees,
the glistening silver birches below him by the river
like elegant and lithesome girls,
the sturdy oaks above him on the hill,
handsome fellows.
And his favourite oak, the big fellow Auld Cruvie
whose bark had a wise, old face.
Everyone around knew Auld Cruvie.

One day Jack watched his old mother
coming up the hill.
She was gathering tufts of wool that
the sheep had shed on bushes and thorns.
From these she carded and spun and dyed
and knitted them into wee ganseys
and sold them in the village
to make ends meet.
She'd brought Jack a bannock and cheese
so they sat on the hillside
and had a picnic together.
'Jack,' she said,
'I had the queerest dream.
I dreamed the oak trees and the birches
rose up and danced and I minded when I woke
my old granny telt me the legend
every seventy years on midsummer's eve
the trees rise and dance.
And Jack,' she said, 'these trees are the guardians
of great treasure under their roots.

So if you are careful and cannie laddie,
ye maun tak some o' their riches when they rise to dance.
But dinnae be greedy. Tak ower much
and ye winna live tae tell the tale.
That's fit granny said.
An tak this, keep it by ye.'

His mother gave him
a long knitted rope of wool
with twelve loops in it she had knitted for him.
Jack put it in his leather satchel
and watched his mother make her way
down the hill to their little cottage.

As the day wore on
and the sun began to set red in the sky
all the birds, as if by an invisible sign,
rose from the trees
chattering and chirping
and cawing.
A wise, old crow, the cleverest of the birds,
alit beside Jack.
'My,' said Jack, 'what's all this stir?'
'This is the night of nights;
the oaks will dance with the birches.
We have till the morning.'
And off the crow flew.

Jack realised there was a dark shadow behind him:
the laird, the Laird of the Black Airts.
The laird did not, as Jack did,
understand the language
of the birds.
'So what was that about?' demanded the laird.
'The trees will dance tonight,' said Jack.

'Ah, just so,' said the laird
who knew the legend of the treasure
buried beneath the roots of the oak tree –
'Tonight!' and then he was gone.

The laird was not long gone, when up the hill
by the light of the rising moon
came Mary, a servant in the laird's castle.
Mary's mother was blind and Jack,
when he had a free moment,
would take the old lady for a walk by the river
and tell her tales and sing her songs.
Mary hurried up to Jack, glanced anxiously around
and said, 'Jack, I have come to warn you,
the laird is pacing back and forth muttering
madly to himself, as if in a kind of fever
and he has a knife in his belt.
I fear he means to harm you.'
'Thank you. Don't fret, Mary.
I'm well able to look after mysel'.'

As the moon rose in the sky
Jack sat on a log, watching
and waiting
and heard, drifting through the air
beautiful, lilting music.
As he sat he heard behind him
the snap of a twig.
Jack turned – there above him loomed
the laird, brandishing his knife.
'Go near Auld Cruvie and you die;
his treasure is mine.'
And just at that moment
they both saw a wonder:
the great oaks rose from the ground,

roots trailing under them,
and began to lumber down the hill.

At the same time, from below at the riverside,
the silver birches began to step, skip
lightly up the hill.
Jack was entranced to see
the ancient oaks
partner the elegant birches
and dance lightly under the
silvery moonlight to the silvery music.

The laird, carrying a big sack,
lost no time in climbing down
into the birth hole of Auld Cruvie
and stuffed his sack full of gold, silver, jewels.
Jack, mindful of his mother's words,
chose the birth spot of a small tree,
climbed down
and, seeing glistening in the moonlight
a gold ring and silver cup
he placed them in his satchel
and a few small treasures for himself.
'Enough,' he said, and made ready to get out
but found that the root hole had sunk.
He was now deep down.
He tried to clamber up the crumbling sides
but could not
when he heard Mary's anxious voice:
'Jack, Jack, is that you?'
'Bless you, Mary,' said Jack,
blessing his
mother in his heart
as he took out the wool rope ladder.
'Catch,' and he threw it up

into Mary's ready hands.
She secured it round a rock.
'Here, Jack,' and he scrambled to safety.
'We'll need to help the laird,' said Jack.
'He's in Auld Cruvie's birth spot,'
and together they hurried
to what was now a deep pit
and shouted down to the laird
but the laird's ears were deaf with greed,
he could not hear or heed the warnings
so busy was he stuffing his sack
full of treasures.

The music had ceased.
Mary watched and heard the great oaks
lumber their way up the hill.
Jack and Mary ran behind some bushes
and saw the oaks hover over
their birth spots
and crash down into the black holes.
The laird and his treasure buried!

Well, as you may guess,
the Laird of the Black Airts
was never seen again.
The new laird, unlike his greedy uncle,
was a good man.
Jack's mother got the beautiful silver cup,
the jewels Jack sold for enough to keep
them safe and well.
Mary got the gold ring,
and you know what that means!
They all lived happily ever after!

The Well of Youth

*This story I heard from storyteller and Church of Scotland
Minister Russell McLarty whom I had known many years
before as one of my pupils when I taught English at the
Royal High School in Edinburgh. I am very fond of the
twists and the lightness in this story, and its conclusion.*

There was, in the Highlands of Scotland,
an old man and an old woman.

It was the bleak and dark time
of the Clearances
when fat factors were greasing their palms,
charging more than they ought
when they collected the rents.

This couple, old Angus and Mairi, were getting on in years.
But they were very, very happy.
They'd had a good life together.
There was one thing only they lacked –
something that had caused them a little sorrow
in the corner of their hearts,
and that was that they didn't have a child.

And they weren't as strong as in their youth;
they couldn't work the land as they used to

and so it was hard for them to pay the rent.

One day, round came the factor.
'The rent, now!' he demanded.
'We're working hard but, as you see,
we're not as young as we used to be.'
'One week!' said the factor. 'You have one week!'
And off he went.

They had very little but, following the old ways,
they always left something for the little people,
the sidh, the fairy folk –
a bowl of milk, a bannock, whatever they had to spare.

That evening, Angus went out
with his gifts for the fairy folk
and there was a little man.
'You're not looking very happy, Angus.'
'No, the factor is demanding the rent
and we have nothing to give him.'
'I know,' said the little fellow, 'but maybe I can help.'
'How can you help?' said Angus.
'Well,' said the wee fairy man, 'I think that you and Mairi
should take a walk to the top of Ben Sidhean
the hill of the fairies,
and go there to the Well of Youth.
Wash your face and sip the water, but only a sip, mind.
Just a sip, one sip.'
And then the little man was gone.

So Angus told Mairi what the little man had said,
'But I don't know if my old legs will take me
up to the top of Ben Sidhean now.'
'Oh well, Angus,' said Mairi, 'the little people are wise
so I think we should follow their advice.'

So early next morning they set off,
Angus with his walking stick,
and Mairi happed in her knitted shawls
to keep her old bones warm.
They made a long day of it.
It wasn't like the days in their youth
when they could skip and scamper
up to the top of the hill like rabbits.

At last they came to the top of the hill,
and there Mairi stood, bent and wrinkled as an autumn leaf.
Angus gazed out over the hills that he had climbed
and loved in his youth.

Suddenly he heard this beautiful, youthful voice
that reminded him of Mairi
when she was young saying, 'Angus! Angus!'
He turned and there before him was Mairi
but as she had been when he met her,
a young woman with red, flowing hair, sparkling blue eyes,
blue as the summer sky, cheeks like apples.

'Mairi! Mairi! What has happened?'
'Angus, Angus, I took a sip, a sip of the Well of Youth.
Angus, take a sip, take a sip!'
So Angus took a little sip and splashed his face.
When he turned around, Mairi gasped to see
the Angus she had met long years ago,
his crinkly, dark hair, his dark brown eyes, sun burnt,
the strong, muscular, beautiful man she'd fallen in love with.
'Oh, Angus! It is the work of the little people.'

They skipped down the hill, and all week long
worked as in the days of their youth.
At the end of the week, round came the fat factor,

knocked at the door and there was Mairi,
radiant and beautiful.
'Where's old Mairi?' he said.
'I'm Mairi,' she answered.
'Old Mairi, it's old Mairi I want to see.'
'I am old Mairi.'
'Get Angus,' the factor demanded. 'Now!'
Suddenly this young man appeared,
a beautiful, strong, handsome young man
with crinkly, black hair.
'I am Angus,' he said.

The factor looked from one to the other.
'Mairi and Angus?'
Just something about them seemed familiar.
'Yes,' said Angus. 'We climbed Ben Sidhean
to the Well of Youth
and took a sip of the water there
and you see what happened!'

The factor didn't waste a moment.
He left, he didn't even collect the rent.
They heard nothing of the factor, nothing at all.
Days passed and he didn't appear.
After a while the people,
though they weren't fond of the factor,
wondered where he'd gone, if a mishap had befallen him,
and someone said, 'I saw the factor.
I think he was climbing Ben Sidhean.'
'Oh,' they said, 'we'd better go and look for him.'
So they took a party of people up to the top of Ben Sidhean,
and looking around saw no sign of the factor whatsoever,
then Mairi heard a little cry.
'That surely sounds like the cry of a baby,' she said.
And in the heather there was a little baby.

Whose baby could it be? They were amazed.
How could a little baby have got away
up to the top of the hill?

Mairi wrapped him in one of her shawls
and they took him back to their cottage.
They asked all around the countryside
whose baby it could be. Nobody knew.
But as Mairi and Angus had always wanted a little one,
and because they'd found him,
they kept the little fellow.

He lived with them and grew to be a very helpful little boy,
kind and pleasant, a singer and a good piper.

The only strange thing about him was that he bore
an uncanny resemblance to the factor.

The Makers of Dreams

As well as being a favourite story to tell, and therefore one I wish to pass on, I have enjoyed using it in workshops with a series of questions relating the events in the story to the lives of the participants, for example, remembering a time of being young and carefree with friends, a time of losing friends, a time of being lost either physically or emotionally. You can extrapolate and invent questions of your own that arise from the story. I have found it successful to have this pursued in groups of three or four with the privacy this confers. In this way, I seek to avoid the trap of preaching, 'and so my brethren, you see the meaning of this story is …' The aim I have is to let people internalise the story and relate it directly to their experience.

Long since, in the time of the old gods, on a day of crisp autumn, some young women were gathering blaeberries on the lower slopes of the Cuillins on the island of Skye. They were laughing and chattering and singing. The boldest and fleetest and loveliest of them climbed higher and ever higher up the slopes of the mountain, seeking the sharpest and sweetest of the blue-ripe berries. Full of dreams, higher and higher she climbed, so caught in the search for the sharpest and sweetest and most perfect little berries that she no longer heard the singing and laughter and chattering of her companions.

A sudden chill ran in the air and looking up she saw, rolling towards her, a blank wall of mountain mist. Alarmed to be alone she turned to find her way back but saw that she was lost.

Through the mist she saw above her craggy shapes of rocks and below, dizzy gullies eddying with wispy apparitions of mist. She dared move neither forward nor backwards, upwards nor downwards.

At that moment she heard the sound of footsteps and saw approaching her, huge ghostly forms, like the legendary giants of the Cuillins. She shrank in terror and could not move.

A sudden flurry of wind made a momentary clearing in the mist and she laughed out loud to see that her companions were a herd of deer, mostly hinds with young calves following at their heels.

These deer seemed unafraid and so she followed behind them as they grazed and moved sure-footed along the craggy ridges. They would, she hoped, lead her to safety.

As if they were obeying a voice from the mountain, they all pricked their ears and set off purposefully along a narrow track. The track led not down but upwards and came to a cave high in the Cuillins.

In this cave were an old man and an old woman seated on two stools gazing into a dark rock pool on the floor of the cave. When the old woman heard the deer she rose to fetch her milking pail and, seeing the girl at the entrance to the cave, she stopped to ask her name and her business in that place.

The girl told how she came to lose her companions and offered the old woman her blaeberries saying, 'Can you give me shelter for this night?'

'For a night?' said the old woman and she turned to her husband and together they spoke in a strange tongue. At length she replied, 'For a night, no, but for a year and a night, yes, we can give you shelter if you will help me with the beast, for now I grow old. The deer will bring you back to the sea at the latter end of the year.'

To this the girl agreed. And the days ran by while she was busy milking and tending the hinds. The old woman taught her too, how to find and gather sweet-scented herbs from the mountainside; thyme she picked on the rock face, meadow sweet and wild mint from the edge of the mountain burns, golden asphodel and bog myrtle from the swampy peat ground.

These herbs the old woman dried and sprinkled on the peat and heather fire. Over this she heated the deer's milk to make croudie. The making of this croudie was the old woman's life.

While she worked at this, the old man sat gazing into the pool in which was mirrored the whole world. When the croudie was prepared he took it and fashioned it into all the shapes and figures he had seen on the pool's surface. This was his whole life. For he and his wife were the makers of dreams.

Each night as the red sun set below the sea foam the old man carried these dreams out to the mouth of the cave and held them up to take colour from the setting sun. Some he held in his right hand, some in his left.

Those dreams from his right hand were airy and light, beautiful dreams full of comfort and promise. Out of the blue heavens they were carried by birds of good omen: eagles, falcons, larks and even the cheeky, little wren. These sweet dreams they carried under the veil of sleep through the whole wide world.

But from the left hand of the old man came nightmarish fantasies, ugly apparitions, dreams full of false phantoms, dreams to deceive. Out of the dark skies, out of the shadowy corries of mist these illusions were borne by birds of evil omen. The smell of carrion was on them, ravens, hoodie crows, rooks and kites. Through the web of darkness they took these deceptions and horrors under the eyelids of world.

When the year and one night of the young woman's service came to an end, the old woman said to her, 'You have served us well.' Then in her strange tongue she spoke to the leader of the herd, a hind grey with age. 'Go well,' she said to the girl, 'your reward awaits you.'

Following the old hind, the deer led her by an easy path down to the seashore, but to no place that she knew. When she tried to walk along the beach the deer huddled round her, preventing her from moving, and all were gazing out over the morning bright sea.

Following their intent gazes she saw coming out of the sunrise a boat of skins, a little coracle, and in it a fair youth. Around his throat glistened a hoop of the finest gold showing him to be the son of a king. She looked upon this prince and he upon her and each thought the other fair. And she loved him.

He beached his little craft and came ashore, his hands outstretched. The deer parted to make a path for him.

'Fair one of dreams,' he said, 'night after night in my father's halls have I dreamed of you, seen your face in this place, so hither I came to seek you as my bride, if you will come with me.'

Already the sun was setting as they sailed towards his father's kingdom in the west. When she became queen of that land, she taught its people the meaning of many dreams and they grew wise.

But much is forgotten.

The Firetail

As a storyteller, it was a revelation and a joy when I came upon the stories in Otta F. Swire's erudite and demotic books collected from the people living in the Scottish islands and western seaboard. Many of the stories she heard from her mother who in turn had heard them from generations of the family on Skye. It was a pleasure to hear a selection of these tales given voice in 2021 by Heather Yule and Bea Ferguson at the Scottish Storytelling Centre. The stories of 'The Firetail' and 'The Dream Makers' are found in The Inner Hebrides and Their Legends, *one of four collections of stories by Otta F. Swire, and are amongst my favourite stories to tell with their evocation of the world of the Celts. Apart from some additions and editing of my own – the way of the oral storyteller tradition – I'm indebted to Otta Swire for gathering these marvellous tales from the folk who told them.*

Long, long ago, all the birds that ever were belonged to Tír na nÓg, the land of the ever young. There they filled the air of these Blessed Isles with colour and song. Only occasionally did they visit the world of men and women to cheer and comfort them with the promise of what was in store for the brave and the wise and the good when they came to that Land of Perpetual Youth in the west, beyond the setting sun.

Beyond all dreams the delight of that land,
A place of fair green meadows,
Of orchards bearing fruit through all the year.
Green, green the trees dripping with wild honeydew,
Crystal clear the tumbling rivers run,
A place it is where beautiful youths,
Hair the yellow of primrose,
Maidens' skin pure as snow
Walk and talk and mingle in the golden colours of the sunset.
The hue of the foxglove is on every cheek.
Their horses are the fairy breed,
Their hounds outrun the wind.
No one speaks of mine and thine,
Mead and wine are never ending,
The feast will never cloy.
Here is no sickness nor pain,
No death or decay.
The music of the soft breeze,
The singing of bright birds
Carry the Ever Young each night
To the sweet oblivion of dreams.

But the price of perpetual youth in these Isles of the Blest was forgetfulness, too high a price for some,
> for those who prized the memory of high deeds,
>> the light in the eye of heroes,
>>> the face of a loved one,
>>>> the cry of a newborn child.

For those who loved to remember and tell of old times, great halls were set aside in the meadows of Tír na nÓg, and in the midst of these halls burned a fire. The fires of Tír na nÓg needed no kindling or tending, were never dull or smoky but burned warm and red with little dancing flames of blue and gold and orange and green. Round the flickering flames these ancients sat telling yarns of old that were strangely, in the telling, ever new. The fire was the centre of their ceilidh of music, story and song, seeming to give pictures to their tales and add a glow of comfort and ease and companionship. This was at a time when fire was unknown to men on earth.

Sometimes the old gods would visit them and tell tales of how it was before the beginning and how it would be in times yet to come, in the times of their children's children. And the birds of Angus Og, the God of Youth, would sometimes sing to them so that the hearts of these ancient ones were young again.

There was at that time, hopping about among all those bright and glorious birds, a little, dull brown bird, unseen among her beautiful coloured companions. This little creature, seeing the glow of the flames, the warmth of the fire, the comfort it brought, the pictures it gave to the minds of the old folk, thought how this treasure would warm and comfort men and women on earth.

So, gathering its courage, this little bird flew into the presence of the gods and the gods listened to her plea. The god who ruled over the Blessed Isles sat in silence for a long time, so long that the little bird began to hop fretfully about from foot to foot and wanted to fly away.

At last the god spoke. 'You yourself may carry fire to the world of men and women, if you can find a living human who is kind and good and brave and wise enough to be the custodian of this great gift.'

And with that he struck a brand of perpetual fire in the little bird's tail. From that time the bird was the firetail. Full of joy, the little bird flew off to find a human who was kind and good and brave and wise enough to have this gift of fire.

As the little firetail perched in a bush she saw a man, and to him she offered the gift of fire glowing and shimmering in her tail. In his ignorance, the man tried to catch and kill her.

Bewildered and afraid, she flew off deep, deep into the shelter of the forest and there asked the owl what she should do.

'Go to the plover, the larks in the high sky and the gulls on the shining sea,' said the owl, 'and ask them to spread news of this gift over all the earth so that a worthy one can be found to receive it.'

This is what the little firetail did.

Soon, from every part came chiefs and champions, hunters and heroes, to the bush in the forest where the little bird sat with her precious gift. The first, a mighty man, stepped forward.

> 'The treasure should be mine;
> the dragon Sevenheads I killed
> with nothing but this naked blade.
> The treasure should be mine.'

At this, a warrior laughed.
'A naked blade!' he scoffed.
'With my bare hands I slew
the Nine Head Serpent of the sea!
The treasure should be mine.'

'Blade and hands?' a hunter growled.
'The play of boys! With nothing but the fierceness of
     my gaze
I quelled the Black and Nameless thing,
the Beast of Fear that walks the dark.
The treasure should be mine.'

'Liar!' shouted the first. 'Braggart!' the second. In a flash, angry words turned to weapons and all around, below and beside the little frightened bird, men roared and yelled and fought.

In terror the little bird flew and flew and flew until, out

of exhaustion, she fell to the ground outside a small cottage. There a girl child picked her up and ran in to show her mother. 'See, the little bird is nearly dead.'

The woman was nursing her sick baby, but she turned and looked at the bedraggled little bird. 'Lay her in the straw,' she said gently. 'Give her water to drink and later I will bring her curds.'

As the little bird lay growing warm in the straw and watching the woman looking after her child and feeding the family and preparing curds, she thought, 'How wonderful it would be if this woman could be the one to receive the gift from Tír na nÓg.'

So when the woman brought her the curds, she asked, 'Are you brave and kind and wise and good? For I have a gift for such a one.'

The woman laughed. 'Oh no, no. I'm just an ordinary woman, a mother. I am too busy digging or sowing or tending the animals or spinning or weaving or cooking or cleaning or looking after these little ones and feeding my husband when he comes home from the hunt. No, I have not time for these great deeds.' And she placed before the bird a seashell of fresh curds.

Suddenly the firetail knew what to do. She was still tired and weak, so she asked the little girl who'd rescued her to bring a few pine twigs. This the girl quickly did. These the firetail fashioned into a nest. When it was complete, she dipped into it her tail, and from a red glow it burst into the wonder of fire, dancing flames of blue and gold and yellow and green.

She had found the one worthy to be the custodian of the gift.

That night, around the nest of flames gathered the family. It gave them comfort and warmth. And as the flames danced in the hearth, their flickering pictures wakened in the family stories and songs and music, gifts from the Ceilidh Halls of the Ancients in Tír na nÓg, gifts to keep the hearts of the kind and good and wise forever young.

And from that time too the air was filled with the colour and song of birds.

The poem appears in 'Oisin in the Land of Youth' from *The High Deeds of Finn and Other Bardic Romances of Ancient Ireland* by TW Rolleston, 1910.

Caolte the Swift

From a lean account of this Celtic story, I was attracted by the brevity, wit and conclusion.

In the misty times from which legends come, the High King of Ireland was seeking the swiftest of runners to report if the foot of any stranger had invaded the shores of Erin and Alba, the ancient Ireland and the ancient Scotland. This was an age of mighty men and wondrous women, of wondrous men and mighty women.

To belong to the band of Fionn McCoull alone, a champion had to be:

Versed in the twelve great books of poetry;
To be themselves skilled in the making of poem and song;
To be buried to the waist in earth and defend themselves with no more than a shield and staff of hazel wood against the spears of nine warriors, and sustain no wounds;
Leap a spar their forehead's height;
To run swift as a deer through the meadows of the morning;
And pass through the forest without rustling a leaf or snapping a twig.

From men of such prowess the High King of Ireland sought a swift runner. From all over the Celtic lands and Celtic kingdoms came champions. And, at last, three contestants remained. From

Brittany, Carnar, so swift it was said that he could leap from Brittany to Cornwall to Cork with three great strides, and that before the sun had risen over the hills of the east.

From Alba, Tormid, so swift that in all contests of speed he was forced to run upon his hands so that other runners had an equal chance, and still at the end he would have time to draw breath and drink a stoop of mead whilst waiting for the others to arrive.

From the champions of the Fianna came Caolte, he who could take a glen at a step, a hill at a hop and Ben Builben at a running leap. He who could run across the meadows of the morning so swiftly that he would not bend the tips of the blades of grass.

And so, these three came before the great King.

'How swiftly can you run,' the king said to Carnar, 'to the sands of the north, the sands of the south, the sands of the east and the sands of the west to see if the footprint of any stranger has invaded the shore of Erin or Alba?'

'Why,' said Carnar, 'as quickly as a cat will slip between the walls of two houses.'

'Not fast enough!' said the High King.

And to Tormid of Alba he said, 'How swiftly can you run to the sands of the north, the sands of the south, the sands of the east and the sands of the west to see if the foot of any stranger has invaded the shore of Erin or Alba?'

'As quickly,' he said, 'as a leaf will fall from a tree to the ground.'

'Not fast enough!' said the High King.

And turning to Caolte he said, 'How swiftly can you run to the sands of the north, the sands of the south, the sands of the east and the sands of the west to see if the foot of any stranger has invaded the shore of Erin or Alba?'

'As quickly,' said Caolte, 'as a woman will change her mind.'

'When will you go?' said the High King of Ireland.

'I have already returned,' said Caolte.

The Sweetest Music

I particularly like this Celtic tale with its characterisation of the followers of the great Fionn McCoull and the answer they give according to their natures. Fionn's answer of the 'music of what is happening' holds the age-old wisdom expressed in the words of Jesus, 'take no thought for the morrow' and his stern-sounding command, 'Let the dead bury the dead.' This accords too with the central tenets of Buddhist teachings.

The legendary Fionn McCoull and his hunter-warriors of the Fianna had spent the day hunting on the high hill and now at last rested on the slopes overlooking the red sun on the western sea.

Fionn turned to his warriors and said to Oscar, 'What, Oscar, is the sweetest music?' At once the great warrior replied, 'The sweetest music is the clash of spear on shield in the hot rush of battle.'

'Hmm, hmm,' said Fionn. 'And you, Caolte, what to you is the sweetest music?'

'The sweetest music,' said Caolte, 'is the baying of the hounds swift in pursuit of the deer on the high hill.'

'Hmm,' said Fionn. 'And Oisin, great maker of words, what to you is the sweetest music?'

'It is the first call of the cuckoo in the springtime,' said Oisin the poet.

'Hmm,' said Fionn, 'and Diarmid, brother of my heart,

what to you is the sweetest music?'

'The sweetest music,' said Diarmid, 'is the ripple of a girl's laughter meeting with her first love.'

And then said Oisin to Fionn, 'What to you, Fionn, is the sweetest music?'

And Fionn replied, 'It is the music of what is happening.'

The Young Hero's Children

Amongst Celtic tales this is a favourite, not only of mine, but of several of the entourage of Scottish storytellers. This egalitarian version is true to the Celtic age in which women, as well as men, were great warriors, like Sgiach, warrior woman of Skye to whom the great Cuchullain came to refine his fighting skills by an epic combat with Sgiach and her daughter. This version is one I have formed from various sources.

Out among the seaward hills of Argyll
Fionn McCoull and his companions of the Fianna were hunting.

Long and hard the run of men and hounds.
They had hunted and killed a deer
and now rested content on the heather hillside
gazing over the cool, green sea.

As they lay, Goll MacMorna, Goll of the one eye,
and that eye sharp as an eagle's,
looked far out to sea and saw
a speck, a fleck on the silver sea,
a nutshell, a war galley.

The men caught up their spears and shields.
'Wait you, wait you now,' said Fionn.
'Not every stranger is our enemy;

no shields hang on the sides of the galley.'

The boat ground into the shingle,
the rowers shipped their oars
and strode over the pebbled beach.
A young man, tall and fair,
a chain of silver and coral round his neck,
strode fearlessly towards Fionn and his hunters.

His eyes rested at last on Fionn.
'You are the great Fionn McCoull,
Chief of the Brotherhood of the Fianna.'
'That I am. What do you wish with me?'
'A great grief is on me,' said the stranger.
'Two sons of mine I have lost at birth, stolen from me.
I am sure to lose the child about to be born
unless I have your help.
You alone of all men can help me.'
'And how if I refuse?' said Fionn.
'I lay upon you a geis,' said the stranger,
'that you shall neither eat nor drink nor sleep before you follow me.'

With that the stranger turned and strode to the shore
where the rowers had pulled the boat into the water.
In he sprang. The rowers bent to their oars,
the boat soon was a nut, a speck, a lost shadow
on the dark of the horizon.

Fionn turned to his men. 'Since I may neither eat
nor drink nor sleep before I follow him, I will.'
'We will come with you,' said his men.
'Not so. Upon myself is this geis laid.
Alone I go. Take our kill back with you
to the Dun of Allan, and by and by I will return.'

Alone Fionn walked along the shore
and there he met with four men and three women,
as if almost they had awaited him. A man stepped forward.
'Greetings to you, great Fionn McCoull,' said he,
'the sun and moon upon your path.
What service can we do for you?'

'Greetings to you,' said Fionn. 'What thing
can you do best in all the world?'
'I am a carpenter. With three strokes of this
worthy axe I can make yonder alder tree a ship!'
A woman stepped forward.
'And what your skill?' asked Fionn.
'I am a tracker,' she answered. 'I can track
the wild duck over nine waves in nine days!'
'And you?' asked Fionn to the brawny man
who stepped forward.
'I am a gripper, and will not let go of my grip
until my arms are ripped from my shoulders,
or what I grip comes with me.'
'And you?' said Fionn, as a lean woman stepped towards him.
'I am a climber, and can climb a thread of silk
tied to the third star of Orion's belt in the sky.'
'And you?' said Fionn, to a man with a stealthy tread.
'I am a thief. Whilst the heron sits on her nest,
I can steal her eggs from under her.'
'And what of you?' asked Fionn of a silent woman.
'I am a listener, and can hear the whisper of
someone at the world's end.'
'And your skill?' said Fionn to the seventh,
a sharp-eyed warrior.
'I am a marksman, and can hit an egg thrown into the sky
as high as my arrow can fly.'

'I thank you all,' said Fionn. 'Come!'

With three blows the carpenter fashioned a boat.
The seven launched it into the sea,
the tracker at the bow, Fionn at the steering oar,
and through the water it sped,
fast as a white-maned steed of Mannanan, the sea god.

The tracker followed the faintest ripple on the water,
and before dark they made landfall.
On the shore was the stranger's war ship.
From a dwelling far into the glen came smoke
from amongst the hazel and the alder woods.
From there, out strode the stranger,
greeted Fionn as if he was a long lost brother.
'You have come!'
'I was hungry, thirsty.
Soon also I shall have need of sleep.' Fionn laughed.
'Eat, drink,' said the stranger,
'and when you have heard my story, sleep.'

A feast was laid – salmon and roast boar, fine heather ale.
Well they ate and well they drank and listened
to the music of the harp.
Then the young man told his tale:
'Seven years ago I wooed and won
and paid the bride price for the woman of my heart
and brought her here.
One year from that day she bore a son
and that very night, through the chimney hole in the roof,
a great arm descended and snatched our child away.
Three years ago, this very night,
she bore another son.
Again, an arm, a gnarled hand, like the brown
root of great tree, came down and snatched the child away.
And now tonight, in the women's quarters,
once more my wife in labour lies.

This is the reason I lay upon you this geis.'

'What is possible to do, we will do,' said Fionn.
'Take us close by these quarters and we will keep guard.'

And so, as night fell, they did.

Fionn himself sat by the fire,
his companions close by outside.
To keep himself awake, Fionn had heated a bar of iron
and drove this into his palm when he felt sleep invade.

At midnight, the child was born.
Hardly had the women announced that it was a son
when, down through the chimney hole,
came a great and gnarled hand to snatch
the howling bairn.
Fionn called the gripper and he grasped the gnarled hand.
That hand shook the gripper like a rat
shaken by a dog,
but still he did not lose his grip till a howl
of rage and agony rent the house,
and through the chimney hole crashed a great arm
torn from the very shoulder.

But, quick as a snake, the other arm darted down,
seized the baby and it was gone.

Great was the wailing and lamenting
in the house of the young hero.
'Before dawn,' said Fionn,
'We will set out and we will never rest
until we have found this child.'

Once more, at the break of day,

to the ship they ran, Fionn at the steering oar,
the tracker at the bow sniffing the air
like a hound hot on a scent.

At sunset, far ahead of them, a speck.
By the last rays of the sun and first rays of the moon
they saw, too small for an island, a rock-built tower
rising straight from the sea, the roof of it
a shining sheen of silver in the moonlight.
They rowed the boat against the rock's sheer face.
Fionn nodded to the climber
who scaled the walls as if she were a fly
and disappeared into the dark.
They waited.
At last she returned and said,
'The roof is of slimy eel skin
or I would have returned sooner.'
'What did you see?' said Fionn.
'Gazing through the smoke hole
I saw a giant, asleep in a bed covered with silk
and sheets of satin, his right shoulder
swathed in bloody bandages.
In his left hand, a baby slept.
On the floor, two small boys played shinty
with sticks of gold, a ball of silver.
By the fire, a wolfhound bitch lay
suckling two pups, one grey and one brindled.'

'Now then,' said Fionn, 'the thief!
Carry him up again with you, on your back.'
And so they went, the climber and the thief.
More than once they went
and they returned with everything –
the boys with the golden shinty sticks and silver ball,
the babe from out the hollow of the giant's hand,

the two pups from the wolfhound bitch,
the silken cover and even the satin sheet
that lay below the giant.

Only the giant and the wolfhound bitch they left.
Then fast as arms could row and sail could blow,
across the waves they flew.
The babe, Fionn wrapped in the sheets of silk,
the two pups by its side.
Fionn was at the steering oar, the listener at the stern,
'The giant awakes!' she said.
'He shivers without his coverlet, he roars in fury.
He wakes the hound and sends her after us.
Make haste! She has a mother's grief
and anger in her for these lost pups.'

The rowers bent to the oars,
but soon they saw the wolfhound coming after,
red sparks flying from her flanks,
her breath hot fire and smoke
and she closing on their boat.

'If she comes near, we will burn alive,' said Fionn.
'Drop one of her pups overboard.'
And so they did. Threw the grey pup into the boiling sea.
And to be sure, the mother took it by the neck
and swam away and grew to a speck in the moonlight dark.

Hard through the night they rowed
and the listener spoke,
'The wolfhound has returned, the giant
commands her to come again, but she will not.
She lays her ears back, growls,
bares her teeth and will not leave her pup.
He curses like thunder and now he, himself, will come.'

'Row for our lives,' said Fionn.

The ship whistled like the wind across the waves,
the oars flashed in the light of dawn.

But then they saw and heard the giant
wading thigh-high through the waves,
water boiling at each stride,
closer, closer, closer he came,
towering above them in the sky.

Fionn put his thumb to his tooth
from where he had the gift of seeing
from Fintan, the salmon of wisdom.
At once, he divined the one place
that could kill the enchanted giant,
a mole in the palm of his remaining hand.

Fionn told the marksman this
and he made ready his bow.
'One glimpse of the mole
and he is dead!' said the marksman.

The giant drew level with the boat,
towering above with his hand outstretched,
he reached to crush the boat, but
in that instant, the marksman drew back his bow.
The arrow sped and pierced the mole.
The giant let out one howl, fell into the bubbling sea
and disappeared.

'And now,' said Fionn, 'once more to the
giant's tower return, where we will take
the brother of this pup and the mother too.'

And so they did, and now the mother
was as quiet as the silent sea
and across that sea, slowly they rowed,
weary, weary, and returned to the shore
of the young stranger with their precious cargo.

The young hero saw them approach and,
with his wife, ran to meet the boat.
When they saw, not just the baby but
both their sons, they wept for joy.
The young hero knelt to Fionn
as if he had been a king.
'What reward will you have?' said he.
'One of these fine pups,' said Fionn, 'is all.'

Great was the feasting and the sport.
Music, song and dance,
feasting on salmon, wild boar and heather ale.

A year and a day they were the guest of the young hero,
and if the last day's feasting was not the best,
assuredly it was not the worst.

When they set sail, Fionn took with him
the brindled and white-chested pup
and called him Bran.
It was his favourite hound.

Only twice in his life was Fionn to weep,
and once was at the death of Bran,
But that is another story.

Arthur and the Hag

This tale has its prototype in Geoffrey Chaucer's 'Wife of Bath' story of the loathly lady, in Child Ballad 31, The Marriage of Sir Gawain, and in the Arthurian tale of the same name. This is an adaptation I made for a performance in Edinburgh's Queen's Hall which places the events on Arthur's Seat with its legendary associations with King Arthur.

The hunt on the slopes of the Seat of Arthur was afoot. Before the swift steeds through dappled forest ran a beautiful white deer till all fell behind but Arthur himself. Into the thickness of the forest she vanished. Arthur dismounted and on foot followed the tracks, came into a clearing and there, before him on a black stallion, a warrior in armour black. At Arthur's breast he lowered his blue, sharp spear point.

'Now Arthur, proud King of the North Britons, you die and I the dark warrior shall take your place.'

'And a poor king shall you be,' calmly answered Arthur.

'Why so? Speak before you die!'

'It is no bravery to slay an unarmed man. And to be a worthy king a man must to bravery add wisdom, wit and honour.'

The dark one laughed. 'Why then, on the honour of a king to prove your wisdom and your wit answer me a riddle and return within these seven days with its answer, or answer with your death at this spear's point.'

'Your riddle?'

'What,' said the warrior, 'in all the world do women most desire? One week!' With that he wheeled and into the darkness of the forest he was gone.

Puzzled, Arthur returned. And on his way asked women of the fields this riddle and many answers did he have. As he rode towards the great stronghold his lady wife saw his approach.

'Why so sad, good Lord, what is the cloud that sits upon your brow?'

The King told her his tale.

'Why,' said she, 'the answer is simple. A good man like yourself is what a woman most desires!'

He was not sure. He asked courtiers, children, ancient crones, and yet at the week's end he was not sure. As he was coming into the forest the way grew darker, damper, and suddenly by the pathway he saw a flash of red, of crimson red. It was a woman's dress. In a song-sweet voice this woman, so strangely alone in the forest said, 'It is Arthur! What trouble sits on your brow, my King?'

Hearing this voice so honey silken sweet he thought, 'This must be a woman of rare beauty,' but approaching near he saw a ghastly sight: a sad misshapen hag, hair limp, scalp patchy bald, pocked and broken skin, one reddened eye and other closed and yet this larksong voice.

'What troubles you, my King?'

'So strangely ugly, and yet a woman,' thought the King and he told her of his peril and the riddle. Like music she laughed.

'It is easy! Come close.'

He leaned close to her acrid breath and in his ear she whispered words.

At once his eyes were bright with hope. 'I thank you,' said he and took his way into the forest.

There in that clearing astride the stallion was the warrior,

ARTHUR AND THE HAG

spear pointed at Arthur's breast. 'And now you die.'

'I think not!' said Arthur and told the words the hag had whispered in his ear.

'How came you by this answer?'

'That is a riddle for you to answer,' said Arthur.

In fury the dark warrior wheeled his steed and in a moment was gone into the thickness of the forest.

As Arthur returned, once more on his way, the flash of red, of crimson red, the musical voice, 'My lord, you are alive!'

'I owe you my life. What boon would you have?'

'On the word of a king, one wish!' said she.

'What you will.'

'I wish the hand in marriage of one of the warriors of your court.'

Arthur was silent, looked upon this hideous form. He thought of his brave, young followers. 'Ask again,' said he, 'land, riches, jewels, men at arms, servants, a great house, what you will.'

'Upon the word of a king, my lord one wish!'

Arthur rode back, and once more his lady saw him from afar. Her heart leapt in joy but then saw how he was bent, downcast in the saddle. 'You are alive my king, my lord, my husband,' said she. 'Why so sad?'

He unfolded the tale of his strange encounter and his word as a king.

'Call your warriors together,' said she. 'I am sure that one amongst them from loyalty to you will take her, however she is.'

Arthur gathered his men and told how things stood and in no way did he varnish the truth of the appearance of this strange woman. The warriors shuffled. The married men blessed their good luck. At last young Gawain spoke. 'For love of you my king, and for that once I wronged a woman, I will marry her however she is.'

So it was that next day Arthur and a companion warrior rode out and came to that same forest path and so once more the flash of red, a beautiful dress and heard that honey sweet voice. 'You have come.'

The companion warrior seeing this frightful form whispered to the king, 'You cannot ask Gawain to marry ... this.'

But already Gawain knelt before her asking for her hand. She gazed deep and deep into Gawain's eyes to see if this were mockery but saw only the light of truth.

So it was that the three rode to the Dun of Arthur, Edin's fortress, once again.

Downcast were the eyes of all the court of Arthur when they saw the sight of this strange woman. The marriage date was set. All the warriors and their consorts attended the feast but there was little merriment. Some quaffed great stoups of mead but most had little appetite to eat. And then the music, the dance.

Gallantly Gawain took his new bride to the floor. In a beautiful bright red dress she was clad, sparkling jewels, but nothing could conceal her shape. The king and others, to make some show, joined the dance.

And then all was at an end. It was time to retire to the bridal chamber. There before a glowing fire sat Gawain gazing into the flames, into his fate and wondering what he had done. And then, silk-soft her voice, 'My lord, time it is for us to retire.'

Whether it was the musical sweetness of the voice, a deep compassion or some inner prompting, Gawain turned and kissed her on her thin, cold lips, opened his eyes and there before him stood a woman of radiant beauty, smiling.

'By this kiss, you have broken half the spell that I am under,' said she.

'Half? Half?' he enquired.

'Yes, half, for I can only be as you see me now by day or by night. Which will you choose?'

Gawain was perplexed. Thoughts played like flickering

fire flames in his mind. At last he said, 'I cannot decide. You choose.'

The chamber rang with the music of her laughter. 'You have broken the spell entirely now. You have given me what every woman most desires – the authority to choose for herself. Now I will be as you see me by day and by night.'

Next morning the company in Arthur's court at the Dun of Edin thought to see Gawain early astir, but it was late in the day that with his radiant, lovely wife he came into their company. And then was there feasting and drinking and dancing!

Oi and Yalasid

I heard George McPherson from the Isle of Skye tell this story at a performance I organised for the Edinburgh International Festival at the time when Brian McMaster was the Director. The form I have given it is the one I feel appropriate to the age and milieu of the story.

In the bright golden days,
when yet the world was young
and the mists of false religion
        had not yet hidden the gods from men,
there lived a lithe, young hunter
            named Oi.

And Oi was the greatest of all the hunters,
for it was said
    he could track down an animal far into the hills
    and bring down a bird with his arrow
        when it was but a speck in the sky.

And his arrows were straight-grained wands
                      tipped with silver.
And Oi lived for nothing but the hunt,
        to spend the days with his companions
        roaming for hours
               through the moors and the glens.

And afterwards – the feasts!
>> Heather ale, birch wine and usquabae.
>>> The feasting went on and on.

And it came one day,
> when Oi was in the mountains,
>> he looked upon Yalasid.
And each looked upon the other,
> thought the other fair.

And from that time,
> Oi had no time for the hunt
>> nor for his companions.
And Yalasid forsook hers as well.
They would spend hours in the glens in their secret places.

But,
> Yalasid was the daughter of Morgai,
>> a woman of great magical powers.
And Morgai was not pleased that
> Yalasid might marry Oi.
He had not proved himself in combat
> and therefore was not yet a hero.
And Morgai thought that Yalasid deserved a hero.

She told these thoughts to Yalasid,
> and Yalasid cried,
'I would rather be a bird in the sky
> singing my song to Oi
>> than not be with him.'

And Morgai looked at her,
> and said,

'Then a bird you shall be
                but no song shall you have.'

And at that moment
                Yalasid turned into a great, white swan.
And she flew over the Duloch
                and landed as close to the house of Oi as she
        could.
And when Oi awoke in the morning
                he could not find Yalasid anywhere.
Though he looked through the moors
                and over the hills
                        and went to their secret places,
                                he could not find her.

He returned to his cottage,
                desolate and lonely.
And from that time onwards he could not think
                                of the hunt,
but only search
        for Yalasid.

And there always,
        flying over his head
                was the great, white swan.
For the swan followed him for days
                over the moors,
                        through the glens.
Finally, one day,
        in a fit of irritation
he drew his bow and shot the swan
                through the breast.

As it fluttered down to the ground
        it landed at his feet

and turned into the form of Yalasid
with his arrow through her breast.

He took her in his arms
            full of remorse for what he had done.
And as he did so, she sang her final song.
She told him that all had happened
                    had been worth it
for this one
        final moment
                in his arms.
And at that,
        she died.

So Oi took Yalasid
    and buried her in one of their secret places
and returned to his cottage and could not
                            be consoled.

Food was like dust and ash in his mouth.

He could not sleep
            for he was deep in remorse.
And at his deepest moment of grief
    Morgai came to him and she said,

'I cannot bring your Yalasid back,
            but if you are willing
                    to turn into the shape that Yalasid was
                        before she died
you will be with her forever.'
            And Oi agreed.
And Morgai wove her spell and left.

And the next morning
>	the companions of Oi came to search for him,
and he was nowhere to be found.

On the waters of the loch
>	were the bodies of two giant, white swans
>		with one arrow between their breasts,
their necks intertwined.

And Morgai took their bodies
>	and buried them at the foot
>		of a cairn of stones covered with turf.

But their spirits had already
>	flown together
to the land of Tir na nÓg,
>	the land of the ever young.

The Lonely Fisherman

I first heard this story from George McPherson of Glendale in Skye and adapted it for an Edinburgh Fringe Festival performance with harp accompaniment by Katie Targett-Adams. We also married the beautiful Selchie Song (Jane Yolen and Lui Collins) to the poetry of my version.

On an island in the Hebrides lived a young
                                                fisherman.
A sad and lonely man he was.
No fisherman would work with him,
no woman would walk out with him.
This was because it was said that
        from his birth
                the Devil had put his finger on him
and the mark blazed red across his face
        from brow to chin.

And so the fishermen said,
        'He is bad luck,'
and the young women said,
        'He is too ugly,'
and so he was very lonely
        in his little cottage by the sea.

In the evening gloom he used to

                wander down to the shore
and come home late into the night
        with only the voice of the sea waves
                whispering in the sand for company,
only the sound of the surge of the sea.
At the fishing he was doing poorly
                for you need two to work the nets
and a hand for the gutting eases the work.

One evening, dark in despair,
                he walked by the shore.
Grey the sea, grey the sky
                and he grey in despair.

As he walked he saw before him on the rocks
                a beautiful woman combing her hair,
                    long, shining, blue-black in the moonlight.
She was naked
                and her back was to him.
Cautiously he came close and close
                and saw lying on the rocks
                      a sealskin.

She was a selchie maiden,
        a seal woman.

Close and close he came and
                snatched up the sealskin.
She turned,
        her great brown eyes filled with tears.
She pleaded, pleaded for her sealskin.

                'No,' he said, 'no, for I am so lonely.'

He told her his tale and she saw his face,

                    the red blaze from brow to chin
                    where it was said that he bore
                        the Devil's mark.

And so out of pity she agreed to go with him to his cottage
                    but more
                        because she wanted her sealskin,
                        wanted to return to her people.

    But though she searched,
        not in the first days or weeks could she find that skin.

    And so they lived together.
                Time passed,
                and her feelings for the fisherman changed,
                changed to a deep, earthly love.
    And they became as man and wife.

    One evening as he was walking alone by the sea
            it seemed that the shifting pebbles whispered,
            voices from the sea whispering:
    'She belongs to the sea; let her return,
            return to her own people,
                the people of the sea.
                Leave her. Let her be free.'

A tear ran down his scarred face into the salty sea.

He returned to his cottage from the whispering sea
                        and said to her:
'I do not wish you to leave
        but I will tell you where your sealskin is
        so that you can return to your own people of the sea.'

But she said,

'No, for I have grown to love you.
             Leave the skin where it is.
                          Do not tell me where it is hidden.'

And the fisherman was happy.
Never in all his days had he known such happiness.

And for fifteen years they lived there as man and wife.

They had three children,
             a boy and two girls.

And after these years
             fate took its play.

One day, the youngest girl, Ailidh,
             the very image of her mother,
found in the shed amongst the nets
             a box, and carefully wrapped in it,
             a sealskin, a beautiful sealskin.
  She was so happy
             she ran with it into the cottage
  and held it out to show her mother.

And at once her mother knew,
             deeply she knew,
                          this was her own sealskin.
  Like the pull of the tide
  a longing filled her to return to the ocean,
       her own kingdom,
             her own sealfolks,
                    to go back to the selchies.
  Like a wild and beautiful
       singing in her ears

she heard voices calling her,
> sea voices
>> calling her back;
the ancient call of the ocean,
> the voice of her own seal soul.
And that call took the blood from her face.

Tears, salt tears ran from her brown eyes,
> and she turned away covering her face
>> in her long, dark hair.

She was torn between her earthly love
> for this kind, loving man,
>> the years of sweet companionship,
> her family,
and the sea love that swam in her blood
> from the beginning of the selchie folk.

She loved her earth family
but like a tide from the beginning of time
> the voice of her sea family
>> was calling her back.

When the fisherman returned that evening,
> he saw in her at once,
>> the change, the sea change in her face.
'You have found the skin.'
'I must go,' she said.
> 'To lose you will be like losing another beautiful skin
> of these fifteen years' growing. But I must return.'

He told her these fifteen years were the sweetest of all gifts,
> more than he could ever have dreamed of.
> But now he knew she must go.

And then together that evening
>> they drifted down to the sea,
>> he himself carrying the sealskin for her.
>> and where they first met, they parted.

And she said,
 'If ever a time comes when the children
 have no longer need of you
>> and you have need of me
>>> come to this place and call
>>>> and I will answer you.'

He returned to his own little cottage and the children.

There for five years he stayed,
> the older boy and girl moved away from the island.

And then came the sorrowful news
> that the ship they were in sank
> and they drowned at sea.

And then his youngest daughter, Ailidh said:
> 'Father I wish to make my own life and to go the mainland.'

So once more the fisherman was left alone in his empty cottage
> with nothing but memories.
And like a grey cloud
> the desolation of loneliness came upon him.

He cared for nothing, not even his work
and spent the days wandering the empty shore,
> looking at the empty sea.

One evening as he wandered by the shore
> in this dark desolation

it was as if he heard the little waves
                       whispering,
whispering with the soft voice of his sea wife:

'Remember, remember,
       if a time comes when the children have no longer
            need of you and you have need of me,
                 come to the place where we first met
                     and call to me and I will answer.'

And to that rocky place he went and called,
       and out of the sea came an answering cry
       and through the waves she came to him and said:

'Come now and join me in our kingdom under the sea,'
       and he stretched out his hand
            and she took it and led him
               down, down, down,
                     into the green depths of the sea.

Down, down into the caverns under the sea,
everywhere shimmerings of green, green light, green shade.
Strands and long leaves of seaweed
     moving gently in the invisible currents of the ocean.
Seagreen grass,
     and gems and pearls scattered on the white sand.
Walls of coral embedded with jewels.
And within furnished with shells
                of every shape and size and colour,
                cushions of moss and giant sponges.

Here, for five years in her sea kingdom,
         they lived in tranquillity
             and found great happiness

> here in her sea kingdom.

They were happy and joyous together.

And then came the news that their daughter Ailidh
> had returned to the island and to the cottage
> with her husband and would soon give birth
> to their first grandchild.

'Even if it is only to hold the bairn in my arms
for a moment,' he said,
> 'I must return to see the child.'
And she said:
> 'For love of you I will return, but if we return,
we lose our immortality.
No more can we enter the kingdom of the sea,
> nor live upon the land.'
'So be it,' said the fisherman.

When they heard the child was born
> they swam together to the shore,
> and taking human form once more,
> walked hand in hand to the cottage door.

They entered and their daughter welcomed and embraced them.

Lying in the cradle was a strong, little baby girl.
The fisherman lifted and kissed her
> and passed the little one to his wife.

She held her, kissed her and placed her back in the cradle.

They each put a pearl on either side of the baby's head,
> a hansel, a gift from the sea.

Then as evening fell they bade their daughter farewell,
>	left the house
>		and together walked towards the shore.

In the morning the bodies of two seals,
>	a male and a female,
>		were found lying on the rocks
>			halfway between the shore and the house
>				and their flippers were intertwined.

The fisherman and his wife were never seen again.

Selchie of Sule Skerrie

The sea and its creatures, from the great whale to the frightening giant octopus and the legendary seal with its reputation of being able to take human form, fascinated me from an early age. From various sources, tales of the sea folk, or selchies, I assembled the following version which I told in the Yukon Storytelling Festival in the 1990s, in Whitehorse. I had been invited there on the recommendation of poet, writer, storyteller and ex-school pupil of mine, Tom Pow. My sources were sung verses of the ballad, Walter Traill Dennison's The Play O De Laithie Odivere, an adaptation of that in a recording and verse form by Gordon Boc, another in the Orkney Tapestry by George Mackay Brown. My telling in the Whitehorse Festival took an hour. As I walked by the river afterwards, I came across a young woman weeping. The cause of her tears I found was the story I had just told which I took to be a tribute to the story itself and to my telling.

> *Baloo, baloo, my peerie wee bairn,*
> *Baloo, a song I'll sing to thee*
> *Of a lady fair wha walked the land*
> *And the selchie man frae Sule Skerrie.*

For this, one of the most ancient stories of the seal people, we go to the far north of Scotland, beyond the knuckle-end of

SELCHIE OF SULE SKERRIE

Caithness, across the stormy Pentland Firth with its racing, dangerous tides and come to the green, flat lands of the Orkney Islands. Pitched in the great Atlantic out to the west of these islands is the rocky outcrop of Sule Skerrie. Here, legend has it and story tells, is the home of the great grey seals; under the sea their kingdom and there, the handsome, grey selchie himself.

But our tale begins not at that rocky outcrop but long ago in the islands of Orkney, those bare islands, layered with history held in the ancient eloquent stones, a legacy of the mysteries of Druid rituals.

In these far past times there lived a young woman richly endowed with castle, lands and servants. With the coming of the autumn, white waves of barley blew in the soft west winds, fat cattle grazed on the fertile fields. This lady was gifted in beauty of form, feature and mind. She was, in the words of one dark suitor, 'the fairest woman in the western world.' Her name was Ingeborg.

For all that, in her heart was a great grief. In the evenings when the castle grew quiet, she would walk from the grey walls and drift down the steep path below the battlements, down to the shore. She would walk to a rock at the far end of the strand and sit on a little ledge, gazing, pondering, grieving. As she gazed out at the dark sea watching the white flecks break on the backs of the waves she remembered:

> The black stallion, her father's
> The white mare, her mother's

She remembered the mist clinging like a shroud round the battlements of the castle
She remembered the moon like the face of a pale and curious ghost peering down

And she remembered the hooves
clattering on the cobblestones of the castle courtyard,
> and the two horses,
> the black stallion, her father's
> the white mare, her mother's

returning riderless from their visit to the dark Lord Odivere.

And the search: she remembered the search tracing the horses' hooves down the steep, winding path to the seashore, down to the tide's edge, where they disappeared under the waves of the dark sea. Three days in the thin sea mist, in the drifting haar, they searched and at last discovered the two bodies,
> sea-soaked and huddled together,
> cradled in a little rock pool,
> rocked gently by the sea like babies,
>> like two cold, dead bairns.

Down to this ledge of rock she would come and gaze at the sea, look at the flashing white manes of the waves and remember:
  the black stallion, her father's
  the white mare, her mother's
and she would listen to the tunes of the lapping waters,
> rustling the little pebbles,
>> drawing them back into the body of the ocean,

and she would fancy herself one of these little pebbles drowning in the peace of the moving waters.

In response to the sea melodies, she would sing her sadness:

> I am alone in these grey walls,
> No friend or kin to comfort me,
> My only rest when here I stray,
> The solace of the endless sea.

As she sang, silently, from the water, one by one came the glis-

tening heads of the great, grey seals and gazed with homesick, hungry, yearning eyes at the land like creatures banished from joy.
And they listened to her song, watched with eyes large and brown.
And she fancied that these eyes too glistened with tears of sympathy as if they knew her sadness.

Often too she would come to the sea for comfort, for rest and for reassurance when her head was dizzy with the flattering tongues of suitors.

> Far and wide her beauty was known.
> From far and wide they came
> coveting her lands, her castle, her riches,
> wanting for their own her beauty, her birth, her body.
> They wanted not her but what was hers.
> Weary she would come to the edge of the sea,
> and there rest on her little ledge of rock.
> She would listen and she would sing:

> > My only rest when here I stray,
> > The solace of the endless sea.

Always as she sang, the great, grey seals would show from the ocean and she would gaze into the warmth of their unblinking eyes. It was as if from the depths of the sea they brought their secret silence and she was comforted and reassured. One particularly would gaze into her eyes, intense and warm, a great, handsome head.

One such night, the moon a slim golden scimitar in the sky,
> a silver crescent on the water
> she finished her song.
One by one she watched the great seals slip like silk under

the surface of the sea and last dove the great one of the dark, handsome head.
And she felt utterly alone.
She looked at the silver moon on the water, a slender knife.
She remembered the white mare, her mother's, the black stallion, her father's.
The two bodies rocked like children in the cradling pool
and the salt tears ran from her cheeks into the salty sea.
She rose from the rocky ledge and walked alone along the shore.

A stranger fell into step with her.
He said nothing.
He walked by her side like a dream man.
She felt no fear, but a strange comfort.
She saw that he was dark as she was fair.

He seemed to know her sadness and said nothing.
Each of three nights when her song was ended and she walked along the shore, he fell into step with her.
The moon came to its first quarter:
'A sad song,' he said.
'A sad song,' said she, 'for a lonely life.'

Night followed night and after her singing he would come.
They would walk along the shore, and as the moon grew full she unfolded to him her story, her sorrow.
    He listened, intent,
        a warm presence,
            like a dream man,
                a man from a dream.
And always when they came to the end of the bay,
he would leave her, turn and walk along the shore into the dark
    and like a dream man, he faded.

A full moon long they walked along the shore together and the dark stranger spoke of making a journey. The moon was a thin cusp when he came to the end of the shore. Ingeborg turned. She took the gold ring that her mother had given her father and she gave it to the stranger. The highest wave of the incoming tide lapped over their feet as he took the ring and placed it on his finger.

> And you hae gien this golden ring,
> A token of your love to me,
> By the full moon's light, by land and sea,
> So surely we must wedded be.

> The surest tide must ebb and flow,
> So surely I maun also go,
> But like the tide I will return,
> Await the coming of the moon.

And with that he left her, like a dream faded and gone.

From that time, every suitor had the scorn on her tongue.
    Their talk seemed shallow,
        their intentions shoddy,
            their trappings gaudy.
She called them fools, she called them fleas. She sent them home with stinging ears, like dogs with tails between their legs.

One night,
'Holla ... a ... a ... h!'
A mighty voice below the battlements.

'I seek out Ingeborg,
the fairest woman in the western world,
a match for the mightiest warrior of the north.'

It was the dark Lord Odivere, a suitor braver far than all the rest,
> great in song
> fleet in dance
> wild and sweet his words in poetry,

a lavish man mighty in battle
and fierce in will to have fair Ingeborg as his bride.

He came with fine horses brightly decked, a gay retinue with red banners blowing in the wind.

He came with lavish gifts of silk and perfume and jewels.

He made her head giddy with words,
> giddy with the swirl of the dance,
> giddy with the stories of distant lands,
> giddy with his overtures of love

but to the proposal of marriage, her answer was always 'No.'

He who had never known defeat in battle would not concede defeat in love.

'I will return, fair Ingeborg,' he sang, 'and you shall take my hand.'

He wheeled his horse and off they rode, a wild and splendid troupe.

Below the battlements his voice rang out, 'Fairest woman in the western world, Ingeborg.'

And with a clatter of hooves they were gone, the horses flashing into the dark.

Odivere would not brook defeat and he brooded, and brooding, his mood grew darker.

At the darkest time of the year, the sun an orange fire on the skyline, on the night of the midwinter solstice, he took himself to the ancient place of the stones, to the altar of the ancient gods and to them he prayed.

At the very cost of his soul he would have her.

O father Odin, before Christ or any god I pray,
    If it cost my soul, lend me your power
      to make fair Ingeborg my bride.

    And he's gaed down on bended knee,
      And vowed a vow upon his life,
    And swore by him that hung on tree,
      To make this lady fair his wife.

Odin lent his dark power, but for such an oath, a burning reckoning would wait in the womb of time.

For now, Odivere was aglow, like a man in flame, a man whose life was charmed.

When next he came to the castle of Ingeborg, he came quietly and alone.
He brought no gifts but the silken words on his tongue, the sweetness of his song, the fleetness of his foot in the dance.
His gaiety bore a spell.
His eyes burned a soft glow.
No one's laughter was more lightsome, no one's wit quicker nor more thrilling.
He seemed to be the very prince of charm, a dark and glowing prince.

His sole devotion was Ingeborg.
And when he sang, the walls of her defence broke down.
He spoke of far lands and of love, sad songs of love, and her eyes filled with tears.
Glad songs, she laughed with him.
Gently he took her hand in the dance and she thrilled to the dark power in his arms.
He charmed her, he wooed her and by Odin's oath, he won her.

Without knowing it, she was the bride of Odin's dark spell.

Soon, from the castle and through the land, rang the sound of wedding bells. Seven days of feasting and drinking, dancing and music and song.
Red banners flew from the battlements, red wine flowed in the drinking vessels and red meat at the table.
Seven days was the revelry.
Flushed red the cheeks of Ingeborg with joy.
Burned red, the face of Odivere with drink, with victory, with defiance.
But it was not long it lasted.

> He boasted long both far and wide
> By Odin's oath his prize did claim,
> Fair Ingeborg to be his bride
> And he in bridal chamber lain.

Long he feasted, he toasted, he bragged and he boasted.

But the feasting over and Ingeborg won. Odivere burned with a restlessness to roam, his blood hot for the battlefield.

He hated the dull, domestic round; of what interest to him the furrowing of fields, the tilling of soil, the harvesting of crops. He was tired of looking at the fat beasts in the fields, listening to the tittle tattle of servants. This was no life for a warrior. These cold castle walls were a prison. He gathered his men.

'We will cross the seas in our longships. We will fight the pagans.' And as an act of defiance he determined, in the name of Christ, to conquer these followers of Odin, the very god by whose oath he had sworn. For did he not bear a charmed life, the bravest warrior in the northern lands? And so he went to war against the followers of the ancient gods.

And Ingeborg felt like a prisoner.
All the laughter of his presence was gone,
her husband, the light and glow,
her love was gone.

She would gaze over the seas where the longships had made their furrows.

Endlessly she combed her long, yellow hair.
Weeks became months, seasons turned and a year passed by.

For days a cold mist hung around the castle, a deep sea haar, and the dark of an autumn night had fallen.

Suddenly the mist broke, the great, pale moon showed from behind a cloud, a voice rang out below the castle ramparts,

'Open! Let me within the shelter of your castle walls.'
'Away! No one sleeps here whilst Odivere is gone,' said the guard.
'From Odivere I come with news, let me in.'

At once the gates were opened.

He was shown into the Great Hall and the Lady Ingeborg came running to hear news of Odivere.
The dark stranger gazed at her.
He knelt before her on his knee.
'I bring you word of Odivere. I left him well.'

With that he gazed at her – intent, warm – with his dark brown eyes and laid upon her lap a ring.

Somewhere a mist was clearing in her mind ... She gazed in

puzzlement into the dark brown eyes of the kneeling stranger.
She looked at the ring upon her lap.

The blood left her cheeks … ghostly pale she grew.

She had her servants prepare a meal.
She feasted him, she welcomed him.

Tables were spread with wine and meat …
And while the servants attended, she pressed him for word of Odivere.
He told her of mighty battles fought and won,
of narrow escapes from death,
of fields of blood and of great victories.

He spoke of Odivere's strength of arm with sword on the battlefield,
of his thirst for wine at the table,
of his appetite for feasting,
of his love for music and song, and he hinted too
how Odivere loved the silken ladies of foreign lands
and had among them kept his own sweet darlings.

When the table was cleared
and when the servants were gone,
and when they sat before the glowing fire of logs,
it was then, when he gazed at her with a steady glow in his eyes,
that the film of inner mist cleared
and she saw as if under the clear moon,
her stranger on the shore.

'Why did you bring me back that golden ring?' said she.
He looked her full in the face, eye to eye, and she felt a surge like the surge of the full neap tide.
And she remembered the water lapping at her feet.

On that ring, in the moonlight clear,
You swore forever mine to be,
And I in grief have gone since then
A lonely man on land and sea.

I never saw a woman's face
But I craved it yours to be.
If they were fair or fleet or wise,
I hungered but to be with thee.

'Why have you not kept the vow of the ring?' he said.
'You know the truth,' said she. 'You know full well what sundered us. It was the dreadful Odin's oath.'
'Come with me,' he said, 'and keep true to the vow of love we made; our vow of love by land and sea, the vow we made under the moon by the sea.'
'I cannot.'
'Come,' he said.
'It is too late.'

He spoke no word but took her hand
And covered it with kisses sweet
And gazing deep into his eyes,
She felt the pull of moon and sea.

She looked then once more into his eyes and drowned in the love that Odin's eye had blinded. The mist cleared. Once more she was under the clear, bright moon, once more on the shore the stranger's voice, like a rustling tide, pulling the little pebbles back into the body of the ocean. And beneath the waves and under the surging power of the sea, she sighed and sank as if she breathed the sweetest air that ever she had breathed.
Once more they walked the shore together.
And then the first edge came from the roundness of the moon,

of the ripening of the barley.

And he was gone as if called by an irresistible tide.

Once more she was alone.

And then with the passing of nine long months from the coming of the stranger, Ingeborg gave birth to a little dark-haired boy, and she sang to her bairn sad lullabies.

> Baloo, baloo, sweet, peerie bairn
> Thou little kens thy mother's pain,
> For I know not thy father's name,
> Nor yet the land that he bides in.

Slow were the days, longer the nights.

And these she'd spend walking the shore, gazing to sea, grieving for her absent love.

And then one night
a strange guest came to her bedside.
'Here I am, thy bairnie's father, although no husband to thy love.'

She wept with joy, and then she took the little child, the little dark child with snow-white skin, with hair dark as a raven's wing. She showed him to his father.

He took him in his arms and then he said,
'In six months I will come again, and I will come with gold for the nurse's fee and take this little one to be my heir.'

> A sweeter man I'll never see,
> A kinder man I'll never know.

SELCHIE OF SULE SKERRIE

> Tell me true what is your name
> And what the land you bide in?

And at once he answered,

> San Imravoe it is my name.
> I walk on land, I swim in sea.
> Among the rank of selchie folk
> I am an earl of high degree.
>
> I am a man upon the land,
> I am a selchie on the sea,
> And when I'm far and far from land,
> My hame it is in Sule Skerrie.

'But how can you take our little boy to such a place?' said she.

> My peerie bairn, wi' muckle care
> Tae Sule Skerrie I'll ferry hame
> Wi's gentle care as e'er we loved
> I'll teach him how to swim the faem.
>
> And when shall I see my bonnie wee bairn?
> You need not lose him from your side
> Whose paws are soot, whose coat is snow,
> But come with me and be my bride.

'I dare not,' said she. 'My husband is a man of blood, a man of vengeance. He will kill both you and our young son.'
'I fear nothing of that,' said San Imravoe. 'In six months I shall return.'

> In six months I will come again,
> For then once more a man I'll be,

> And take my bonnie selchie bairn
> Into the joys of Sule Skerrie.'

And she saw his eyes grow dark,
a turning tide, and in a moment he was gone,
his words echoing in the night.

And so once more she waited. Once more she walked the shore alone.

She turned her father's golden ring against the bright full moon and spoke the name, 'San Imravoe, San Imravoe, return to me.'

Night after night she walked the shore which had been the place of grief and the place of joy.

With the passing of six months, as he promised, he returned.
He came with gold and silver from the ocean floor,
gold and silver from the wrecks of ancient ships.
'I've come to fetch my bonny bairn home,' he said.
Her eyes flowed with tears.

> 'I'll wed thee with this golden ring
> And bide beside thee all thy life.'
> 'Too late, you would not when you could,
> The time is past to be my wife.'

And so she took the golden chain, the golden chain that Odivere had given her as a wedding gift, and she put it round the baby's neck.

> 'Wear this for thy mother's sake
> Thou peerie bairn of land and sea,
> And when the tide and seasons speak,
> Then you shall bring it hame to me.'

Together they walked to the shore and in he waded, taking with him the little baby.
The moon was agleam on the water.
Gently then, San Imravoe swam out into the sea and underneath the waves.
And then two heads emerged into the silver of the moon,
one great, handsome head, dark, glistening, the other white as snow.
And then they were gone.

For Ingeborg, once more the days were long, longer the nights and often of an evening she would walk alone by the sea, waiting, watching, hoping.

And then at daybreak one morning came the cry,
'Boats! Boats, ahoy!'
With boisterous clatter, Odivere returned.

The long ships laden with booty,
tongues freighted with tales of triumph,
victorious, Odivere boasted he bore a charmed life.

'The fairest woman in the western world for the bravest warrior of the north.'
Had he not taken and sworn Odin's oath? Had he not slaughtered Odin's followers?
Was his life not charmed?

'Do I not bear a charmed life?' said he to his silent wife.
He did not see the pallor beneath her skin,
nor hear the shallow flutter of her breath.
'Here is the wife I won by Odin's oath.
His followers I have conquered.
We shall feast, have stories, wine, meat, dancing and song.'
So there were days of feasting, drinking, music, but when

the feasting, the drinking, the music was over, once more he wearied of the tepid taste of castle life,
the dull domestic round, the slow cattle, the fields, the sheep, the dull husbandry of land, furrowing the field, tending the beasts,
tilling the soil, the prattle of servants.
It wearied and chilled his blood.

And so one day he called a hunt: an otter hunt on the shore. And he himself walked by the shore. Suddenly he found a small seal, fine and fair its fur, and with a warrior's practice and skill, he struck a huge blow where he knew it would kill: on the flat of its face against its nose.
With a low and awful sigh, it lay over, dead.
Snow-white its coat, black as soot its paws.

'Ahh,' said a follower, 'a prince, a prince indeed,
a royal seal, a princely seal, white as snow its coat,
black as soot its paws. And what is this fine, golden treasure around its neck?'

Odivere was silent. Not a word he spoke.
Black were his thoughts, thunderous his blood.
Silently he carried it home like a baby and laid it before the fire in the Great Hall of the castle.

'Call down my wife!' he ordered the servant boy.

'Now,' said he, 'explain this fine riddle. What a prize I have found.
A chain of gold I have won from the sea. What say you? You are silent.'
'My ain bonny bairn,' she said, 'my sea child, my son.
Curse the blood of your hand.'
Then she threw her hands around the dead white seal, held

it like a nurse.
'My bairn, my selchie bairn,' she cried.

'What fine games have you played when I was far from home?'
'No finer games than you,' said she. 'No woman was born for a cage
while you would wander far and wide and do whatever was your will.'
'I thought you would be true to me,' he said.
'How true to you when I was won by false oath?'
'You have been false,' said he.
'No more than you, strutting like a cock with silken ladies,
squandering what by rights was mine in other sheets.
May demons torment your soul for all eternity. Take this token of my curse.'
She snapped the chain from around the seal pup's neck
and threw it in the face of Odivere.

In the dark of a high tower, he imprisoned her behind a door of iron,
the very guards forbidden to speak one word to her.
A day was named to have her burned alive.

Below her, Ingeborg could hear her servants prepare a fire and stake to burn her.
She longed for San Imravoe as she gazed out to the sea.

'In a red fire I am to burn. Hear me, San Imravoe, hear me!'

And far out to sea, in the kingdom of the great seal,
San Imravoe heard her plea.

> Come selchie folk and swim with me,
> We'll raise the giants of the deep.

On the day before she was to be burned and the huge fire waited,
a great cry from the men arose:
'Whales! Whales! Whales, ahoy! Whales in every bay and voe.'

Odivere and his men ran to the boats
with a noise that would raise the dead – a whale hunt!
All day they rowed.
All day they hunted, and always they were led to sea
by the great monster whales.
Yet never a whale that day did they kill
but returned with aching bodies and blistered hands, and then:

> They were surprised, you may be sure,
> For open wide was every door.
> And the door to the tower lay on the floor,
> The Lady Ingeborg was far and gone,
> By mortal eyes was never seen.

The rage of Odivere: a fire
that scorched the very marrow of his bones.
It was the curse of breaking Odin's oath.

The Sound of the Surge of the Sea

This is my adaptation of another story by George McPherson who lives in Glendale, Isle of Skye. I have introduced it with 'The Canadian Boat-Song' and woven in the lullaby 'Smile in Your Sleep'.

From the lone shieling of the misty island
Mountains divide us, and the waste of seas –
Yet still the blood is strong, the heart is Highland,
And we in dreams behold the Hebrides.
(Canadian Boat-Song, anonymous)

[1]Hush, hush, time to be sleeping,
Hush, hush, dreams come a-creeping,
Dreams o' peace and o' freedom
So smile in your sleep, bonnie baby.

He was only a boy of seven
    and he lived in his own sweet, green glen
        on the Hebridean island of Lewis,
the land where his people had lived
    for generations out of mind and time.
There he played and ran his heedless days
with his companions

---

[1] Song: 'Smile in Your Sleep' lyrics written by Jim McLean to a traditional tune.

by the stream of the brown trout,
and when the moon came
> out of the mouth of night
he listened
> in the flickering flame of the peat fire
to music and song and the stories
> of the old seanchaidhean and cailleachan,
> > the bearers of the great tales of old.

To the boy the glen was the whole world
and always, night and day,
> he could hear
> the sound of the surge of the sea.

He was only a boy of seven
and he did not understand
> when the dark word came to the glen
> > that they were to be evicted.
> He did not know the meaning of the word.
They were to be thrown off the land of their fathers
> to make way for sheep.

Once our valleys were ringing
With sounds of our children singing,
But now sheep bleat till the evening
And shielings lie empty and broken.

He did not understand when
> three weeks later torches were put
> > to the roofs of their homes
> they were taken from their houses
> > and put into a ship in the bay.

We stood heads bowed in prayer
While factors burned our cottages bare,

The flames fired the clear mountain air
And many were dead in the morning.

Where was our proud highland mettle,
Our men once fearless in battle,
Stand now cowed, huddled like cattle
And wait to be shipped o'er the ocean.

He thought that when the sun shone again
                out of the mouth of morning
he would return to
       his own sweet green glen
         and the sound of the surge of the sea.

Instead,
   with his little brother and two sisters
     they were confined like prisoners below deck
                      in a cramped berth
        six feet long
        three feet wide
        eighteen inches high.
And for his father and mother, the same area
        six feet long
        three feet wide
        eighteen inches high.
And for six long weeks they
          sailed towards America
confined in the airless dark,
     a living nightmare
    of disease and despair and for many, death.

But always in the darkness the boy thought
       they would surely return
      to see his own sweet green glen
     and hear the sound of the surge of the sea.

At last they landed in Nova Scotia
                New Scotland
where the promise had been
            of land and work.
But there was nothing
               but broken promises
          or slavish work
               for a pittance of pay.

And still the boy thought and dreamed
           of his own sweet green glen
                   and the sound of the surge of the sea.

So the family struck off inland
            and trekked westward,
cleared the land of trees and made a farm
and there in Canada the boy worked and grew to manhood
still hearing from his father
        the songs and tales of his native land

               and in his dreams he saw forever
                  his own sweet green glen
           and heard the sound of the surge of the sea.

At length he left the farm
     worked in the forests as a logger
     worked in the great steel mills of America
         on the railways
               wherever he could find a job.
And then at last,
           when age was coming upon him,
           he gathered what money he had put by
       and made the voyage back to Scotland,

> to Lewis, to the port of Stornoway,
> and walked from there
> > to the glen of his childhood.

Everything was changed.

No longer were children at play
> by the stream of the little brown trout.
> There was no smoke from the chimneys
> > of the little black houses.
No stories, music or song
> by the flickering peat fire.

The glen was still green
> but the glen was empty of people, of laughter,
> > of love
and the old man sat down at the shore
> gazing at the ocean
> that all these years ago
> had taken him from the land of his people.

No use pleading or praying
Now gone, gone, all hope of staying
So hush, hush, the anchor's a-weighing
Don't cry in your sleep, bonnie baby.

And there he determined
> > would be his grave,
and there he composed a song
> > in the Gaelic tongue of his childhood.
He called it: An Ataireachd Ard,
> The Sound of the High Surging Sea.

I give you the words in translation:

An Ataireachd Ard

The eternal surge of the sea
The sound of the high surging sea
The roar of the open sea
As I heard it when I was a child
Without changing, without pity
The sound of the shore wave
Shooshing over the sand.

In the western woods
I would not ask to stay forever
My mind and my desire
Were always on the hollow of the sea-bay
But those who were generous in deed
In friendship and happiness
Have been scattered without shelter
As a flock of birds
Gets up before an enemy.

But I shall not travel from you now
I shall no longer move from your company
My age and my colour
Are bringing to mind
The shortness of my days
The time to me to be sleeping
In the cold and in the sleep of death
Make up my bed, make up my bed to the
Sound of the high surging sea.

Hush, hush, time to be sleeping,
Hush, hush, dreams come a-creeping
Dreams o' peace and o' freedom
So smile in your sleep, bonnie baby.

The Iron Cold Winter

The following wild tale I heard from the Irish storyteller John Campbell.

Patrick and Margaret were a lovely couple. The neighbours would say, 'What a nice couple they are up there on the hill; you never hear a word of anger, you never hear them disputing or anything of that kind. They always seem to be in perfect agreement. There's never such a thing as the throwing of ugly names, or the throwing of cups or saucers or insults. No, not at all. Lovely, lovely people.'

But that was before the coming of the iron cold winter. It settled itself on Ireland and everything was frozen, everything was at a standstill. The little puddles were frozen, the little streams were frozen, the ponds were frozen; there wasn't a thing stirring in the landscape. And of course, it was very hard to get anything in the way of game.

Then one day, Margaret turned to Patrick and said, 'Patrick, I'm pinched with hunger, so I am. There's nothing to eat in the house. And why is there nothing to eat in the house? Because you've brought nothing home at all! Not a rabbit, not a fish, not a fowl.'

'Well now Margaret,' said Patrick, 'it's very difficult to get anything just now, so it is. The ground is frozen, the rivers are frozen. Nothing seems to be stirring. How can I provide anything at all?'

'You get yourself out of this house,' she said, 'and take your ugly face with the long nose on it with you. Out you go, and here's your boots!' She threw his boots on to the floor by the door.

Patrick went outside and he looked around. Nothing was moving. Nothing was stirring. He thought, 'What am I going to do to get my face back into the house?' Then he thought, 'The village priest! That's the idea. Now the village priest would have a gun. If I had a gun, I could shoot something for the pot.'

So he made his way down to the house of the priest. Now what Patrick didn't know was that it was a new priest. But although he was a new priest, he was an old man. So Patrick went and he knocked on the door of the priest. The priest shuffled to the door.

'Oh,' he said, 'are you one of my parishioners?'

'Yes, I am,' said Patrick. 'I wonder if you could help me?'

'Oh, certainly, certainly,' said the priest. 'Come in. Come in and take a little warming whisky.' In Ireland in those days the priests were very nice.

So they sat down together and the priest said, 'Now what's your name?'

'Patrick.'

'Well now Patrick, how is it I can help you?'

'Well, I wonder if you've got such a thing as a gun?'

'A gun?' said the priest.

'Yes,' said Patrick. 'It's my wife, you see.'

'Patrick, Patrick,' said the priest, 'I could not give you a gun for that purpose, that would be murder.'

'No, no, no,' said Patrick, 'it's not to shoot my wife. She's thrown me out, told me to take my long nose and my ugly, old face out of the house until I can bring something back – fish, flesh or fowl. So I thought if I had a gun, I could shoot something for the pot.'

'Well,' said the old priest, 'yes, I've got a gun, but the problem with this gun is it's a very old gun.'

'What kind of gun is it?' asked Patrick.

'Oh,' said the priest, 'it's a muzzle loader.'

'A muzzle loader?'

'Yes. Now what you do is you get the gun and you place it against your knee like this and the barrel will be in the air. See? Then you've got to get a bit of wadding. You push this down the barrel with the ramrod. Like this, see? Then after that, you get the gunpowder and you pour it down the barrel and you stamp it down, good and firm, with the ramrod. Then you put in another bit of wadding. Then, and this is the most important part, you put in the shot. This is what is going to get you your dinner, Patrick, and get your ugly ... get your face back into the house. Then you stuff in another bit of wadding and push it down very firm with the ramrod. Then you're ready! Have you got all that?'

'Umm, I think so,' said Patrick. 'I think I've got it.'

'There's just one more thing,' said the priest. 'You must remember to make sure you take the ramrod out of the barrel before you fire it, or I'm not sure what would happen!'

So Patrick took the gun and he was ready to go out and shoot something for the pot, but it was an iron cold winter: nothing was stirring, not a rabbit, not a hare, nothing living on the face of the earth. So he came down to the edge of the mill pond. It was a big, big pond but it was frozen over. He thought, 'There's nothing stirring, nothing to shoot.' Then he looked up into the sky, and what did he see – he saw, in the distance two great, big, fat ducks, flying through the air. He thought, 'That could be our dinner tonight! We could even invite the neighbours to join us. Now, what was it? The wadding, the ramrod ... the shot. Down with the wadding, down with gunpowder. Then the ramrod. Then another piece of wadding. Down with the shot, down with the wadding. There we go. Push down with the ramrod.'

Now the birds were flying exactly over the millpond, so he took up the gun ... and fired! BOOM!

He'd forgotten to take the ramrod out of the barrel. There was an explosion you could have heard several miles away and Patrick was catapulted backwards. He landed, soft as you like, on top of a great, big mountain hare. Broke his fall, killed the hare. 'Oh, this will be in the pot tonight! It will be jugged hare, tasty as you like.' He clasped his hands and raised them to the sky and there he saw a miracle – the ramrod had impaled the two ducks. They were whirling down through the air, just like a parachute. Down into the middle of the millpond.

'Now, my hearties, I will get you,' said Patrick, 'but I'll need to cross this ice. It looks pretty thick.' So he began very carefully, in his big, tackety boots, across the ice and right enough, he got to the middle of the millpond and there was the ramrod, straight through the two ducks. He pulled the first duck off the ramrod, stuck it in his bag. He pulled the other duck off the ramrod, stuck it in his bag. 'Mother Mary, be praised!' Then he looked down and he saw the ramrod had gone through the ice and pierced the heart of a great, big salmon.

'Oh!' he said. 'What a meal we'll have tonight. When Margaret sees me tonight, there'll be hugs and cuddles. Now I need to get this fish out of this pond.'

So he began to stamp at the ice with his great, big, tackety boots. The ice was flying up in splinters. Then a great, big shard of ice came up, sharp as a dagger, and cut his throat, cut his head clean off.

But Patrick was a quick-thinking man. He took hold of his head, pushed it down on to his neck and, because it was so cold, it stuck. 'That was a close shave, right enough,' he said.

On he went, dig, dig, dig. At last, he managed to pull out this great, big salmon. 'Oh, you beauty,' he said. 'Praise be to God.' Into the bag went the salmon.

Home he went, and his throat was so frozen, it was stuck fast.

'Well, there you are Patrick,' said Margaret. 'Did you get

something for the pot at all?'

'I did,' he said. And he pulled a big duck out of his bag.

'Ooh!' she said, 'come on in, come on in. What a feast we'll have tonight.'

'Wait a minute,' he said. And he pulled out the second duck.

'Ooh!' she said. 'Another duck!'

'It is indeed,' he said. 'Just for you, lovely one of my heart.'

'Enough of your blarney,' she said. 'Come in now and get warm.'

'Wait a minute,' he said. And out of the bag he pulled the hare.

'A hare!' she said. 'We can have that skinned and gutted and roasted for tonight. A feast. Come on in, will you.'

'Wait a minute,' he said. And he pulled out a great, big salmon. 'The king of the sea for the queen of my heart.'

'Enough of your blethering and blarney,' she said. 'In you come and let's have a feast. I'll start preparing, plucking these birds, skinning the hare and gutting the fish. You just go and sit and warm yourself by the fire.'

So Patrick sat down by the fire. Now because it was warm, the ice around his neck began to melt. He was in great danger of losing his head and dying there and then. Margaret looked round and she said, 'Oh! What's happened, Patrick?'

'My head's coming off!'

But she was a quick-thinking woman, and she was also a great seamstress. She got her needle and thread and said, 'Now you stay still.'

'I can't do anything else!' said Patrick.

She pushed his head down on his neck and stitch, stitch, stitch, stitch. And she stitched his head back on his neck.

'There you are, Patrick,' she said.

'Thank you, Margaret, you're the queen of my heart. Now we'll invite the neighbours in …'

And of course, they also invited the old priest, and they had a fine feast and a fine story to tell.

Jack and the Silver Shilling

This story I found was always a big favourite when I told it to children in Primary 3 or 4, seven to nine-year-olds. I first heard it told by the inimitable Stanley Robertson in his uncompromising northeast of Scotland Doric dialect. He took as much delight in it as his audience, reliving Jack's good intentions, failures and ultimate triumph.

On a hill in the Highlands of Scotland, there was a great house and in that house there lived a very rich man. He had money, he had everything he could need and he had a daughter that he loved very dearly. But this daughter, she never smiled, she never laughed and she never spoke. And so for all his money, he was very, very sad and nobody could get his little girl to smile or laugh or talk. And so he was not a happy man.

Now in the village just below the hill, lived Jack and his mother. Jack loved his mother very, very dearly and although his mother loved Jack, she was certainly in no doubt that Jack was, as some people would say, not the full shilling. He wasn't just the brightest coin. But he was very well-intentioned. And one day Jack said, 'Mother, I'm very, very hungry.'

'Jack,' she said, 'I'm really sorry, we just have no money left and there's nothing in the house to eat. I really don't know at all what to do.'

'Maybe,' he said, 'I could get some work. I could get a job.'

'What kind of work would you get, Jack?'

'I could go up to the farm and ask if I could get work on the farm.'

'Well, Jack, you could try if you like.'

And so Jack set off at once, very happy.

The farmer saw Jack coming. He knew Jack very well, as people do in a village, and he thought, 'What would Jack be doing here, I wonder?'

Jack appeared and said, 'Er, my mother and me have not any money. I'm very hungry and I was wondering if I could get some work.'

The farmer said, 'Jack, you know farm work is hard work and often you've got to be very careful with what you're doing.'

'Oh, I could work hard,' said Jack.

'Well, I'll tell you what, Jack, I will give you a trial, alright? Today we're howking tatties.'

'Howking tatties?'

'Yes, we're lifting the potatoes out the field, shaking the dirt off them, we're taking the tops off and we're putting them in the basket.'

'Oh,' he said. 'I could do that.'

'Well Jack,' said the farmer, 'we'll give you a try if you like.'

So Jack went into the field and to everybody's amazement he was howking the tatties out, he was taking the tops off, shaking the dirt off and throwing them into the basket. At the end of the morning he'd quite a pile there, and the farmer said, 'Jack, that is wonderful. That's all the work we're going to do today. I tell you what though, Jack, I'm going to give you a silver shilling for your work.'

'Oh!' Jack says.

'Now you be careful, take care of it as you go.'

So Jack took the silver shilling in his hand, and he was walking along the way down the road home when he came to a river. He was looking into the river and he saw this beautiful trout. Jack knew you could guddle a trout, you could tickle a trout, and that way he thought, 'I could guddle that trout, tickle that trout and I could take that trout home and then we'd have a silver shilling and we'd have a trout for our tea.' So anyhow, Jack bent down and unclasped his hand to tickle the trout. The only problem was, it was the hand that was holding the silver shilling, so the shilling was caught up in a current and floated away. Jack couldn't see it and of course the fish swam away too.

When Jack came home, his mother said, 'Well, Jack, you're not looking very happy. Did you not get any work today?'

'I got work at the farm and I got paid a silver shilling.'

'Oh,' she said, 'Jack, that is wonderful.'

'I lost it.'

'Jack, how did you lose your shilling?'

'Well, I thought I could guddle a trout for our tea and …'

'Jack, you tried to guddle a trout with the same hand that you had your shilling in!'

'Yes, Mother.'

'Jack, Jack, Jack, you've no more brains than you was born with! Tomorrow, if you get paid, then what you should do, Jack, is put it in your pocket. Have you got that?'

'Yes, put it in my pocket.'

So the next day off Jack went, and the farmer was very pleased to see him. They were howking tatties again and he was whipping the tops of them, shaking off the dirt and by the end of the day, he had a great pile of potatoes.

The farmer said, 'Well, Jack, that is wonderful. I'll tell you what I'm going to give you today, Jack. I'm going to give you a jug of milk.'

'Oooh, a jug of milk!'

So the farmer gave Jack the jug of milk, and of course Jack went off and he thought, 'Oh, my mother said, "put it in your pocket".' So he poured it into his pocket; it poured all down his leg, away on to the ground.

When he came home his mother said, 'Well, Jack, how did you get on today?'

'I got paid a jug of milk.'

'Oh, that's grand, Jack.'

'Yes, I did just like you said, Mother, and I put it in my pocket.'

'Jack, Jack, Jack,' she said. 'You've no more brains than you was born with! If you get paid next time, remember to carry it on your head.'

So the next day, to cut a long story short, Jack was helping the farmer to clean out the byre. He was doing wonderful work, and at the end of the day the farmer said, 'Today, Jack, I'm going to give you a pat of butter, freshly made.'

On the way home, Jack held the pat of butter on his head, just as his mother had said. Now it happened to be a hot day, and the butter melted through his hair and ran down his face. When he came home, his mother hardly recognised him.

'Jack, is that you?'

'Yes, Mother.'

'What has happened to you?'

'I got paid a dod of butter, Mother.'

'And you put it on your head, didn't you Jack? Jack, Jack, Jack, you've no more brains than you was born with! If you get paid tomorrow, mind you wrap it in wet leaves to keep it cool.'

Well, the next day, Jack went back to the farm and he worked hard all day shawing the neeps. And at the end of the day the farmer said, 'Jack, I saw your mother today and she said that you're troubled with mice, and so I'm going to give you a little kitten, Jack, and the kitten will get rid of the mice for you.'

'Ooh!' Jack said.

So he got the kitten and he remembered what his mother had said. He wrapped it in wet leaves to keep it cool. And of course, the kitten miaowed and miaowed and scratched and scratched and at last scratched its way out of Jack's hands and was gone. So Jack came home.

His mother said, 'Well? How did you get on today, Jack?'

'I got paid a kitten to get rid of the mice that's in the house.'

'Jack, you didn't wrap it in wet leaves did you?'

'Yes, I did. I wrapped it in wet leaves and it ran away.'

'Jack, Jack, Jack, you've no more brains than you was born with! If you get paid tomorrow, put it on a lead to bring it home.'

The next day, Jack went back to the farm and helped with sweeping out the byre. At the end of the day the farmer said, 'Well, Jack, I'm astonished – I've never seen the byre looking so clean. Today I'm going to give you a nice, big ham to take home to your mother.'

Jack remembered his mother's words. He found some twine, tied it around the ham and pulled it along behind him all the way home. All the dogs in the village followed behind too and gobbled at the ham until Jack was pulling nothing but a bone.

When Jack got home, his mother said, 'Well, how did you get on the farm today, Jack?'

'I got a nice, big ham for our supper,' said Jack, 'and I pulled it behind me on a lead, just as you said.'

'Jack, Jack, Jack,' said his mother, looking at the bone, 'you've no more brains than you was born with. Get it right for once – whatever you're paid tomorrow, carry it home on your shoulders, Jack.'

The next day when Jack arrived at the farm, the farmer said, 'Jack, you've done a good week's work, you've worked very hard. I know it's a good, long way for you to walk from your house up here, so I'll tell you what I'm going to do; you're not going to work today at all. And for your pay this week I'm going to give you a donkey.'

'Oh, a donkey!' said Jack.

Well, Jack looked at the donkey and the donkey looked at Jack. Then Jack bent down and with great difficulty he tried to lift the donkey on to his shoulders. He started to make his way home, and the donkey was hee-hawing and was such a weight. So Jack thought that he'd take a shortcut home, past the big house.

The rich man's daughter was standing there at the gate, and when she saw Jack trying to carry the donkey on his shoulders, she smiled and then she laughed out loud. Her father heard her and said, 'Mary, Mary, you're laughing! You're smiling!'

'Yes, Daddy,' she said. 'Look! Look!'

'You're talking too!' said her father, and he looked where she was pointing, through the window. He saw Jack struggling along with the donkey on his shoulders and he said, 'Jack, what are you doing?'

'I'm carrying this donkey home,' said Jack.

'Jack, you don't carry the donkey. The donkey should be carrying you! Get on the donkey and make your way home that way. But before you go, come and get some food for you and your mother. And if you want to visit us any time, you're very, very welcome.'

So Jack rode home on the donkey, with plenty of food as a gift from the big house. His mother saw him coming and she said, 'Jack, where did you get that donkey?'

'I got it for my pay today,' he said.

'And where did all that food come from, Jack?'

'I got it for trying to carry the donkey on my shoulders, just like you told me. And when she saw me, the girl in the big house laughed so much that her father gave me all this food.'

'Well, Jack,' said his mother, 'maybe you've a few more brains than I thought you had.'

Queen With the Cold, Cold Heart

This tale, brilliant for children and to warm up any audience, I first heard when I was on a wonderful storytelling trip to New Zealand in the company of three eloquent storytellers: our New Zealand hostess and chaperone Liz Miller, carrying her ubiquitous chihuahua; Nan Gregory, a feisty Canadian, and my brother spirit, the Irish-American Jay O'Callahan. It was Liz who told this tale and what follows is my attenuated version. It is essential to compel the audience of whatever age to repeat the words and actions as invited. The storyteller needs to be clear, insistent and bold in this demand to get the full fun and engagement.

This is the story of the queen with the cold, cold heart.

Now first of all let me tell you the characters in the story, and of course you have to take part in this story. And so, with each character there is a sound. We have the queen with the cold, cold heart – brrrrrr, brrrrrr (shiver with cold – that is your part). Then we have three princesses: one who has a bad, bad cough – kaaf, kaaf, kaaf; one who has a bad cold and therefore a sniffle – sniff, sniff, sniff (wipe your nose); and one who is beautiful and very, very sad – aaaaaaaaah (mournful sigh, hand on heart). And there is, of course, in this story an evil, evil wizard. For him, you'll rub your hands – heh, heh, heh (evil laugh). There is a guard at the castle who raises a hand and says, 'Halt! Who goes there?' and then

QUEEN WITH THE COLD, COLD HEART 215

there is, of course, the horse – clip clop, clip clop (whinnying sound). And no story is complete without the handsome prince, who raises his hand high and says, 'Ah-haaaaa' (in greeting). So every time these characters appear, you will make their appropriate sounds and actions.

Once upon a time, there was a queen with a cold, cold heart (brrrr). One day she looked out and saw the snow was falling deep because the land was under a spell and everything was frozen by the power of the evil, evil wizard (heh, heh, heh). The ponds were frozen, the streams were frozen, even the waterfalls were frozen, and the snow was falling deep. So the queen with the cold, cold heart (brrrr) thought, 'No one can rescue us unless the snow is cleared to make a path.' So she said to her three princesses, one with the cough (kaaf, kaaf, kaaf), one with the sniffle (sniff, sniff, sniff) and the one who was beautiful but very, very sad (aaahh), 'Go out and make a path through the snow!'

So the three girls went out and began to shovel the snow, and in the distance they heard very quietly clip, clop, getting closer, clip clop, closer still, CLIP, CLOP – a horse, and it came to a halt (whinnying sound). And on the horse was the handsome prince (Aha!). He gazed upon the three daughters, the one with the cough (kaaf, kaaf, kaaf), one with the sniffle (sniff, sniff, sniff) and the one who was beautiful but very, very sad, (aaahh). And for some reason – no one knows what the reasons are for these things – he fell in love with the one with the sniffle (sniff, sniff, sniff).

And so he went to the palace where the guard raised his hand and said, 'Halt, who goes there?'

The prince answered, 'It is I, the handsome prince (Aha!).' I wish to see the queen with the cold, cold heart (brrrr).'

'Very well,' said the guard. 'Pass.'

And he came before the queen with the cold, cold heart (brrrr).

'Who are you?' asked the queen.

'I am the handsome prince (Aha!) and I wish to marry one of your daughters.'

'Which one?' asked the queen with the cold, cold heart (brrrr).

'The one who seems to have a bit of a sniffle (sniff, sniff, sniff).'

'No,' said the queen, 'no one marries my daughters until the land is cleared of this spell that has been put upon it by the evil, evil wizard (heh, heh, heh).'

'I will rid the land of the spell because I am the handsome prince (Aha!).'

'Very well,' said the queen with the cold, cold heart (brrrr). And she went to the back of the palace and said, 'I will help.' And there was a huge chest of drawers. She opened this great drawer (groaning, creaking sound) and inside that drawer was a smaller drawer (groaning, creaking sound) and inside that an even smaller drawer (creak), inside that a smaller drawer (squeak), inside of that a tiny drawer (eeaak) and inside that there was a bottle.

This she handed to the handsome prince (Aha!) and said, 'If you sprinkle the contents of this on the evil, evil wizard (heh, heh, heh), you will break the spell.'

'I will break the spell, because I'm the handsome prince (Aha!).'

'Good luck!' said the queen with the cold, cold heart (brrrr).

And so off he went, clip, clop, clip, clop. But in the meantime, the evil, evil wizard (heh, heh, heh) was gazing into his crystal ball and he saw approaching, clip, clop, clip, clop, the handsome prince (Aha!). And the prince arrived at the stronghold, where the horse halted (whinnying sound). And the evil wizard (heh, heh, heh) took out a great bolt of lightning and – shuuuuuft – threw it at the handsome prince (greatly enfeebled sound) who was now greatly enfeebled. Meantime, the evil wizard (heh, heh, heh) got ready to throw another bolt of lightning at the handsome prince (Aha!) but at the very last moment the handsome prince (Aha!) opened the bottle and – chuut, prrrr – poured the contents over the evil, evil wizard (heh, heh, heh). At once the evil, evil wizard (heh, heh, heh) grew smaller and smaller and smaller, and the prince (Aha!) at last took him, shoved him into the bottle and pushed the cork down firmly.

That was one story that was told, but there is another story that is told and I believe that it's the true story. In it, the evil, evil wizard (heh, heh, heh) grew smaller and smaller and smaller until he became ... a light bulb! The handsome prince (Aha!) was amazed because in these days, of course, there was no such thing as a light bulb. However, he put it in his saddlebag and off he rode, clip clop, and he returned to the palace once more (whinnying sound).

He went to the guard who said, 'Halt! Who goes there?'

'It is I, the handsome prince (Aha!).'

'Ah!' said the guard. 'Pass.'

And he came before the queen with the cold cold heart (brrrr).

'Did you destroy the evil, evil wizard (heh, heh, heh)?' she asked.

'Yes!' said the handsome prince (Aha!) and he brought out the light bulb.

'Is that the evil, evil wizard (heh, heh, heh)?'

'I think so,' said the handsome prince (Aha!).

'Take him to the dungeon!' said the queen, and four strong men took the light bulb to the dungeon down a dark staircase, badum, badum, badum, badum, down more steps, badum, badum, badum, down some more steps, badum, badum, badum. They came to a dark, deep dungeon and there they put the light bulb in a box and closed the dungeon door (clang).

Immediately the queen with the cold, cold heart no longer had a cold heart, the princess with the sniffle no longer had a sniffle, the one with the bad cough no longer had a cough and the one that was beautiful but very, very sad was now beautiful and no longer sad and, as you might expect, the handsome prince (Aha!) asked the princess who no longer had the sniffle if she would marry him. And we don't know what her answer was because she was a great explorer and thought of travelling the wide, wide world. What do you think she did?

But the story does not end here because years and years later, not very far from where I live in fact, there is an old, old castle. One day two workmen, two Scotsmen, Jimmy and Jock, went down into the dungeon of that old castle and suddenly Jimmy said, 'Hey Jock.'

'Aye.'

'Jock?'

'Aye?'

'There's a box here.'

'Well, what kind of box is it?'

'I don't know, just a box.'

'Ah, well, I think you should open it.'

'Ey, well, I don't think that's a good idea.'

'Why not?'

'Well, it may be full of erm, you know, filthy things, erm, worms and things like that.'

'You should open the box. It could be full of jewels and gold and we'd be rich men.'

'Well it could be full of dynamite … and we'd be dead men.'

'Listen to me, I think you should open the box.'

'I've got a better idea.'

'Aye, what's your idea?'

'You open the box!'

'Alright, you stand back, I'll open the box. Are you ready?'

'Yeah, I'm ready.'

'Are you sure?'

'Yeah, I'm ready.'

'Alright, I'll open the box.'

So he opened the box, wheee. Suddenly a light went on. Wooooooooooh, it was steaming cold, cold, cold. And you know and I know that after all this time it was still the power of the evil, evil wizard (heh, heh, heh).

'Ooh, I'll close the lid again.'

'Let's have another wee look.'

'Aah, alright, let's have another wee look.'

Wheeeu, wheeeu, wooooooh, it was cold, steaming, steaming cold.

'I'll close the lid.'

'Eh, Jock?'

'Aye, yes.'

'I know what we could do with the box.'

'What could we do with the box?'

'We could sell it!'

'Who'd want to buy it?'

'People who wanted to keep things cold.'

So Jock and Jimmy sold the box and it was the very first refrigerator in the whole wide world. And that is the end of the story of the queen with the cold, cold heart (brrrr).

The Little Squirrel

This story I adapted from Ashley Ramsden's telling of the adventures of a chipmunk so as to make it more appropriate to Scotland where there are grey and red squirrels. I found this story a success when children participate in the actions and the repetitions.

It was harvest time,
and Mummy Squirrel said to Little Squirrel,
'Are you feeling brave? I'd like you to help me.'
'Yes, Mummy. What can I do? What can I do?'
'Well, Little Squirrel, now is the time to gather nuts for the long, cold winter.
Can you help with that?'
'Yes, yes. Where do I have to go?'
'You must go through the forest, up the tallest tree,
along the longest branch over the dark pool,
and there you'll find the hazelnuts.'
'I'll do it Mummy! I'll do it!' said Little Squirrel, and off he set.

He walked a little, skipped a little and ran a little until he met the big owl in the tree.
And the big owl looked down and said,
'Hello, Little Squirrel, what are you doing here in the deep, dark forest? Are you not afraid?
After all, you don't have my *sharp claws* to protect yourself.'
'Um … no, no, I'm not afraid,' said Little Squirrel.

'I'm gathering nuts for the winter and I'm feeling very brave.
But I have a long journey, through the forest, up the tallest tree,
along the longest branch over the dark pool,
and there I'll find the hazelnuts, so I must be on my way now.'
'Good luck, Little Squirrel,' said the owl.

Little Squirrel went on his way.
He walked a little, skipped a little, ran a little
until he met the red fox.
The fox looked at Little Squirrel over her long nose and said,
'Hello, Little Squirrel, what are you doing here
in the middle of the deep, dark forest?
Are you not afraid here all on your own?
After all, you don't have my *sharp teeth* to protect yourself.'
'Um ... no, no, I'm not afraid. I'm ... I'm ... not afraid,'
said Little Squirrel.
'I'm gathering nuts for the winter and I need to go through the forest,
up the tallest tree, along the longest branch over the dark pool,
and there I'll find the hazelnuts. I must be on my way now.'
'Good luck, Little Squirrel,' said the red fox.

'Why does everyone keep asking if I'm afraid?'
said Little Squirrel.
But he set off, and he walked a little, skipped a little
and ran a little
until he met the rabbit, who twitched her long ears and said:
'Hello there, Little Squirrel. What are you doing here,
all alone in the deep, dark forest?
Are you not afraid?'
'Afraid of what?' said Little Squirrel.
'Afraid of ... IT!'
'Of "it"?'
'Yes, you know, the THING in the dark pool!
Did no one tell you about the THING,
the THING in the POOL?'

'The THING in the POOL?
No one told me about the thing in the pool.
I must gather the nuts for my mummy before the long winter.
I have to go through the forest, up the tallest tree,
along the longest branch over the dark pool,
and there I'll find the hazelnuts.'

'Good luck, Little Squirrel,' said the rabbit.

Little Squirrel set off, but now more slowly.
He walked a little, he skipped a little and he ran a little
until he came to the tallest tree in the forest.
He scampered up until he found the longest branch,
and then he started to walk slowly across.
The deep, dark pool was below.
'I wish Rabbit hadn't told me about the THING in the POOL.'

Halfway across the branch, he stopped and looked down.
There it was!
'Arghh! The thing in the pool! The thing in the pool is
looking at me!'
But Little Squirrel was very brave, and he thought,
'What can I do?
What can I do?'
So he made an ugly face to scare the thing away.
'Arghh! The thing in the pool made an ugly face!
What can I do? I'll get a stick.'

So Little Squirrel found a stick
and shook it fiercely at the thing in the pool.
'Arghh! The thing in the pool shook a stick too!
What can I do? I'll get a stone.'
So Little Squirrel found a stone and threw it into the pool.
But the thing in the pool threw a stone too.
Little Squirrel turned around and he ran and he ran and he ran,

past the rabbit, past the fox, past the owl,
and he didn't stop running until he got all the way home.

'Did you get the hazelnuts?' asked Mummy Squirrel.
'No, no ... because there was a thing in the pool!'
'A thing in the pool?'
'Yes. It made an ugly face at me,
it shook a stick at me, it threw a stone at me.'
'Oh, a thing in the pool,' said Mummy Squirrel.
'Well, we really need those nuts for the winter,
so you'll have to go back.'
'Go back? Go back?'
'Yes,' said Mummy Squirrel, 'but *don't* make an ugly face
at the thing in the pool, *don't* shake a stick
at the thing in the pool,
and *don't* throw a stone at the thing in the pool.'
'What am I to do then?'
'Smile at the thing in the pool.'
'Smile?'
'Yes, smile.'

And so Little Squirrel set off once more.
He walked a little and skipped a little and ran a little,
past the owl, past the fox, past the rabbit,
all the way to the tallest tree.
He scampered up and slowly crept along the branch
and in the middle he stopped
and he looked down into the pool,
and there was the thing.
So he smiled.
'Oh! The thing in the pool smiled too!'
So he went on and collected the hazelnuts
and walked back along the branch and smiled
and waved at the thing in the pool.
The thing in the pool smiled and waved back.

'The thing in the pool is my friend!'

And then he walked and he skipped and he ran
past the rabbit, past the fox, past the owl,
all the way home.

He gave the hazelnuts to his mother.
'Mummy, Mummy, the thing in the pool is my friend!
It smiled at me, it waved at me.
But who is the thing in the pool?'

And what do you think his mummy said?
Do you know who the thing in the pool is?

Star Apple

This story is fun. I saw Liz Miller in New Zealand telling it with great success to a class of eleven-year-old pupils in a primary school we were visiting and it is an equal success here. You will need to remember to take a red apple and a sharp pen knife to cut the apple, crosswise, at the end of the story. It is wise to try cutting another apple from the same batch before your visit to check you have a nice star. Not every apple has a well-defined star in its centre. It adds to the fun and suspense if, when you cut the apple, you do not show its two halves at once. You need to conceal the apple till the end ... I used to produce it magically out of my sporran!

Once there was a wee girl called Sally. She was bored. Couldn't think what to do.

'I've nothing to do!' she said to her mother.

'Nothing? Why don't you play with your wee doll?'

'Done that!'

'Well, what about that colouring-in book your auntie gave you for your birthday?'

'Done it, finished it.'

'What about your new jigsaw puzzle?'

'Done it!'

'Well, Sally,' said her mother, 'I'll give you something to do. I'd like you to find for me a little, red house with no doors and no windows and a star inside. When you find it you'll get something nice to eat.'

'Where will I find it?'

'That's your puzzle, a treasure hunt. Off you go.'

So Sally set off and called on her friend Jimmy who lived next door.

'Jimmy, I'm going on a treasure hunt. I've to find a little, red house with no doors and no windows and a star inside. When I find it I'll get something nice to eat. Would you like to help?'

When Jimmy heard there could be something nice to eat he said, 'Sure, Sally, I'll help.'

And off they set.

'Let's visit my granny,' said Sally. 'She's been everywhere and she knows everything.'

They rang the bell on Granny's door and soon out she came, a spry old lady with twinkling, blue eyes. 'Sally, and a friend! What brings you to my door this fine day?'

'This is my friend Jimmy and we're looking for a little, red house with no doors and no windows and a star inside, and when we find it we'll get something nice to eat.'

'Och,' said Granny. 'A little, red house with no doors, no windows, a star inside, and if you find it you'll get something nice to eat. That's a riddle indeed.'

She scratched her old, grey-haired head.

'Well, the church has a star at Christmas but it has doors and windows. No, I don't know, but go and ask the farmer. He is a wise man and has been here, there, up and down and everywhere.'

So off to the farmer they went and found him sitting on his tractor.

'Oh ho, you two! What are you doing here?'

'We're looking for something.'

'I hope you're not looking for trouble!'

'No, we're looking for a little, red house with no doors

and no windows and a star inside, and when we find it we'll get something nice to eat.'

'Oh,' said the farmer. 'I've been up and down and round about many places but I can't think what that would be. But if you ask the wind, it might tell you.'

'Where will we find the wind?' asked Jimmy.

'Top of the hill,' said the farmer, and off they ran fast as could be.

At the top of the hill was a tree and there, under the tree, they stood and together shouted into the wind. 'We're looking for a little, red house, with no doors, no windows and a star inside. If we find it we'll get something nice to eat.'

There was a puff of wind and Sally, who was a quick catcher, caught something that fell out of the tree. She clasped it in her hands, hiding it from Jimmy. 'What is it? What is it?' asked Jimmy.

'It's a little, red house with no doors and no windows, but I don't know if it has a star inside.'

'Let me see!'

And Sally showed Jimmy the apple.

'I can find if there is a star,' said Jimmy. He produced a penknife and cut the apple crosswise through the middle.

'Let me see, let me see,' said Sally. Jimmy showed her the two halves and there was not one ... but two stars.

'And now we've got something nice to eat.'

Archie Beag

From a short paragraph in a story collection, I was so taken by this tale that I transplanted it to a family of traditional west coast Scottish pipers.

Well, there was in the Highlands of Scotland
a famous family of pipers, the McCrimmons of Skye,
who for many years had a college that was renowned
throughout the Highlands and Islands and beyond.
But this is not that family.
This story is of a family called the Campbells,
and they too were great pipers.
One after another they seemed to inherit that gift,
and so whenever a little baby was born into the clan
people would be very curious to see how he looked,
and particularly they would want to look at his fingers.

Well, little Archie Campbell was born
and was called after his father, Archie,
so he was known as little Archie, or Archie Beag.
His parents were immediately curious when he was born
to look at him, and indeed, his fingers were moving.
They were long, skilful, supple fingers,
and he had a narrow hand. He could be a spectacular piper.

But as time passed, it wasn't the music of the pipes

that interested little Archie;
from an early age, he was astonishingly adept
and nimble with his fingers,
not picking out a tune,
but picking a pocket, a pouch, or a sporran.
It wasn't long until he wasn't popular amongst his people,
so he decided to take his skills to Aberdeen.

Now you may have heard that Aberdeen folk
have a reputation for clinging to their money.
They're thought to be rather tight-fisted
(not that I ever found that!).
Archie went to Aberdeen and he was picking pockets,
he was picking pouches, he was picking purses
and there wasn't a watch he couldn't snip
from a person's waistcoat with his long, skilful fingers
and his long, narrow hand.
But he wasn't long in Aberdeen
before people became wise to him.
They were not fond of saying farewell to their money,
and it looked as though he might find himself an early grave
or a quick end on the gallows.

He decided he would leave and go somewhere
where the people weren't quite so clever,
and so he decided to go south to London,
where he found the people weren't quite as quick
as those in the north.
He soon was lining his pockets with his long, narrow hands
and his skilful, supple fingers
in the marketplace, in concert halls.
He could wheech off a gold watch or steal a pouch
before anybody could sniff the air or blink an eye.
In no time he was well off.

One day he was in a great crowd of people in the marketplace
when he saw drifting towards him with a lilting walk,
a beautiful woman with long, red hair and radiant, blue eyes,
and a soft and golden tongue.
She approached him and said,
'Excuse me, sir, if you could give me the time of day?'
Well, he had, of course, a gold watch
that he'd got by way of the trade.
He looked at the watch, told her the time
and engaged her in conversation.
'Well,' he said, 'Do you live or work round about here?'
'Oh, well, I do work around about here, after a fashion.'
She thanked him profusely for the time, and he said,
'I hope we'll meet again.'
'I hope so too, sir,' she said, and he realised that she came
from the beautiful green island of Ireland.
'And what a thing,' he thought to himself,
'beautiful things are in Ireland,
and beautiful things come out of Ireland.
How the time passes,' he thought.
But when he looked for his gold watch,
the one he'd acquired by way of the trade,
it was gone.

He looked in his pocket; his pouch was empty.
He couldn't believe it.
He searched all his pockets. Empty. Not a penny.
His gold watch vanished into thin air.
He was dumbfounded. But he realised, of course,
where his watch and where his money had gone.

So every day he looked around the marketplace to see
if he could see the beautiful Irish colleen.

Then one day, he saw her.

There she was, asking the time
from a great, fat, prosperous-looking man
who was obviously, like Archie, captivated by her beauty
and didn't notice when her long fingers,
slippery as an eel,
wheeched into his pocket and pulled out money,
then snipped away his gold watch,
thanked him courteously and off she went on her way.

Well, Archie followed her, tapped her on the shoulder
and she turned round with a bit of a fright,
but for all that she was quick.
'Ah,' she said, 'how nice to see you again, sir.
I do remember you.'
'Och well,' said Archie, 'I'm not surprised.
You won't be having any difficulty
telling the time these days.'
'Oh, but what would you be meaning by that, sir?'
'Well,' he said, 'let's just cut a long story short.
I lost my watch the day I met you.'
'Oh, did you, sir?'
'Yes,' he said. 'You'll be making good use of it I suppose.
But anyhow, it looks as if you're in the same trade as I am.'
'Oh,' she said, 'Is that it?'
'Well, what a good thing it would be ...'
And she finished the sentence.
'... if you and me were to work together.'
'Exactly!' said he.

And so they went into business together,
and there was no concert hall, marketplace or public gathering
where, working as a team,
they weren't making a huge profit.
They made plenty of money, and then one day she said,
'You know, the great skill you have in your fingers,

and the great skill I have with mine,
would it not be a fine thing if we was to be married,
and would it not be a fine thing if we had a little one,
and would that little one not be
one of the wonders of the world in our business?'

And so soon they were married
and it wasn't long until she was expecting a little one.
And there he was, a beautiful, little, red-haired Archie Beag.
But as they looked at him,
their joy and their pleasure turned to dismay,
for the poor, little fellow was deformed.
His right arm was bent up across his chest
and his little fingers were tight closed together,
and there was no way they could unclasp his arm
or his clamped fingers.

They were paralysed.
This was a severe blow to their hopes.

But they were well off and so they tried doctor after doctor.
At last they found a world-famous paediatrician,
a man who had a great reputation working with little ones.
He looked into the little boy's eyes,
'Oh,' he said, 'what an intelligent look the little one has.'
He felt his pulse. 'That's a fine, strong, healthy pulse.
'The blood's flowing well. He seems to be perfectly normal.
In fact, he looks very intelligent for his age.
And look, look how his eyes are perfectly focused
on my gold watch.'

And right enough, the little one's eyes glinted and fixed on
the gold watch
with a great look of intelligence.
'I think I'll have a little experiment,' said the specialist.

He took out his chain and began to swing his gold watch
> like a pendulum
> in front of the little one's eyes, back and forth,
and right enough, the little one's eyes followed it,
one way, then another, until the pendulum stopped,
and at that moment the little one's hand unclasped
> and reached out, his fingers opened
> and he grasped the gold watch,
> and from his hand dropped
> the midwife's gold wedding ring.

> 'That's our boy,' they said.
> 'Our old age is secure.'

Erchie Campbell

Noo a'body kens aboot the McCrimmons,
weel kent for their piping generation efter generation.
Nae sae weel kent wis the fame at the piping
o' my ain clan Campbell fowk.

They were grand pipers and sae it wis that wan Erchie Campbell
wis born intae the faimlie o' skeelie pipers,
fowk sah he had the lang, soopple fingers.
Haurdly hid he taen his first braith, fin they were moving
and grasping the shawl.

'O, that's oor laddie,' they said,
'the lang, soopple, skeelie fingers for the piping.'
But nah, the wee laddie wis scarce a toddler,
fin he wisnae pickin oot a tune,
but pickin pooches, pittin his haunds tae ither ploys.

There wisnae a pocket, purse or pooch
that he couldnae rieve, no a watch he couldnae snick wi
they skeelie fingers an the lang, narra haund.
It wisnae lang for him tae need to seek ither airts
for his skills, so he took his trade in aboot Aiberdeen.

In yon airt it wis lean pickin he had in the pooches and pockets
an it wisnae lang afore they canny fowk jaloused

fit he wis aboot an he wis in fell danger o the gallows.
So he thocht tae ging tae London toon
whaur fowk were nae that canny or crafty,
an och but he lined his pooches there wi his lang, narra haunds
and skeelie fingers.
At merkat or concert he could sneck aff a gowd watch or rieve
a pooch afore onybody could sniff the air
or blink an ee.
In nae time at a' he wis guy bien and weel aff.

Noo, aye day he wis in a muckle thrang of fowk in the merkat
fin a bonnie, bonnie quinie,
an Irish lassie, speired the time fae him.
He tellt her fae a muckle gowd watch he had come by
in the way o' his trade.
He was muckle taen with this sonsie lass,
the bonnie, big, blue een, the lang, black hair.
She thankit him real coothie like
an it wisnae till she had vanished intae the thrang
that he fand his oon pooch was tim.
His siller was gaen. He couldnae credit it.
He howkit in his pooches. Tim. Empty. Nae a bawbie.
Wi his gaud watch vanished intae thin air. Pure glamourie.
He was dumbfoonert.

Weel, ilka day he keekit aboot the merkat place to fin her
an a' day he saw her speirin the time fae a great, muckle mannie
and fin he wis tellin her the time, Erchie saw her lang fingers,
skeelie as an eel, ripe in the pooch o the mannie and
than she thankit him coothie-like and gaed on her way.
Erchie followed her, tapped her on the shooder
an she turned roond wi an awffa fleg.
But for a that she was guy and quick and said,
'Ah, whit would you be wanting, kind sir?'
'Ach weel,' said Erchie, 'I micht be wanting my watch,

but I micht be wanting to pay my respects
tae a quinie wi sicht lang, skeelie, supple fingers.'

An tae mak a near cut o the tale,
they were guy taen wi ain inither
an gaed intae business thegither
an soon were bien an weel aff.
Soon they were merriet and agreed
that wi the skills at their finger ends
a bairn wid be a warld's wonder at the trade.
Soon a bairnie they had, a bonnie, wee loon he wis,
but their plaisure turned to dismay
for the puir, wee cratur wis deformit,
his richt airm bent intil his chest,
his fingers ticht closed thegither
his airm clamped thegither against his breist.
Nae way could they move airm or fingers:
he was paralysed, an awfy dunt tae their hopes.

But sin they were bien an weel aff they sought yin doctor
efter the ither
an at last fand a warld famous mannie
a mannie who had a great name for working wi bairns.
Weel, he keekit intae the wee loon's een and said,
'This is a very intelligent boy.'
He felt his pulse.
'This is a fine healthy boy, the blood's flowing well in his arm.
He looks most intelligent for his age.
See how his eyes are focused on my gold watch.'
An, richt enou, the wee loon's een glinted on the gowd watch
wi a sair intelligence.
The doctor took out his chain and began to swing his watch
like a pendulum, and richt enou, the wee loon's een
glinted and followed it to an fro
and syne the wee bent airm straightened oot

towards the watch.
The fingers opened oot tae grasp it
and that meenit doon drapped the midwife's gowd wedding ring.
Ah, were they no cantie for the wee loon
had inheritit their faimlie gifts.
Their auld age wis secure.
'That's oor laddie,' they said.

The Water of Life

One of the great love stories of Scotland and Scots folk is our passion for usquabae, the water of life, John Barleycorn, the poetry in the bottle, the whisky.

Even a man of the cloth, a sixteenth century Scottish minister had this to say:

Whisky helpeth digestion,
Quickeneth the spirit:
It keepeth the tongue from lisping,
The teeth from chattering,
The throat from rattling,
The stomach from wombling,
The guts from rumbling.

The great Scottish writer James Hogg, the Ettrick Shepherd said, 'If a body could just find out the exac' proportion and quantity that ought to be drunk each day, and keep to that, I verily trow that he might leeve for ever, without dying at a', and that doctors and kirkyards would go oot o' fashion.'

So my tale today is of two lovers, whisky lovers, the two old friends, Hamish and Angus.

This companionship was baptised in whisky; the golden liquor lent fluency to their tongues in the courting days, put fleetness to their feet in their dancing days and gave

THE WATER OF LIFE

philosophy and poetry to their minds in their advancing years, particularly half down the bottle in the wee, small hours of the morning.

On one such night, well into the golden malts, the topic turned to death, and Hamish said, 'Angus, if I should die before you, would you be good enough to pour a bottle of malt over my grave?'

'A *whole* bottle? said Angus.

'Yes.'

'Well,' said Angus, 'you wouldn't mind if I just pass it through the kidneys first?'

The years tumbled on, and then one day Hamish came to visit.

'There's your dram,' said Angus.

'No, thank you,' said Hamish.

'It's a fine malt,' said Angus.

'No, thank you.'

'Hamish, if you're not well, this will be your cure.'

'The Devil is in that glass,' said Hamish. 'It is the ruin of a man. It will destroy body, mind and soul.'

The trouble was Hamish had got a sudden, serious attack of a particular brand of religion. He was a convert and drink was the Devil. Already you could see the signs of abstinence: the mouth grew tight and grim and mean, his face narrow and pinched, his demeanour sour.

And he went off preaching round the land on the evils of drink and eventually returned to give a talk in the village hall. Angus took his seat at the back to hear his old companion.

'Now,' said Hamish, in his new ministerial growl, 'drink is death. It destroys a man's health, it destroys his family, steals from his pocket. It is of the Devil. Just look you here.' Whereupon he produced a wriggling earthworm. 'Now watch you this.' He poured a glass of water, immersed the worm and pulled it out a few seconds later, still wriggling.

He poured whisky into a tumbler and dropped in the

worm. A few seconds later he pulled it out, straight, stiff, dead. Instant rigor mortis. Held it triumphantly aloft. 'You can draw your own conclusions.'

From the back of the hall came the voice of his old friend Angus. 'Yes, if you drink the whisky you will never suffer from the worms!'

Well at last the bottle was empty. Time passed and old Angus was dying. He had gathered a great reputation for wisdom and wit. The family gathered round to see if perhaps he would utter one last memorable word.

His lips moved ... but no utterance ... not a sound. His wife poured a little water into a glass, wet her finger and applied it to his lips ... a little movement ... no sound.

She poured some milk into a glass, thinking this might help. Wet her finger ... touched his lips ... a little movement ... no sound.

She was not one to approve of the liquor, but this called for extreme measures. She poured a little whisky into the milk, dipped in her finger and applied it to the lips of old Angus.

A beatific, little smile appeared on the face of the dying man, and with a sigh he expired with these immortal words: 'Don't sell that cow.'

Hiro the Gambler

I love this Japanese story and loved the way it was told to me in New Zealand by my Irish-American great storytelling friend Jay O' Callahan. I can still hear his voice, which echoes into my own telling of this fun tale.

Hiro was twenty-four years old. Hiro was short and dusty. He was always a mess; he was always with his friends and he was always throwing dice and beating them. 'Ha! Seven! Did it again. Ah, hu, hi, he, seven! Did it again. I am the best, you are the worst. Ha, ha, ha ha, pay me, pay me, pay me!' He would drive his friends mad.

One day they said, 'All you do is talk about yourself, take our money. If you are so great why don't you go up the mountains and beat Tashaka the god?'

Hiro said, 'I will do it. Ha, ha, ha, seven! Did it again. I'll do it. Seven, I'll do it.' He thought to himself he would go halfway up, sit on a log, come down and say he'd done it, beaten Tashaka.

They knew he would go halfway up, sit on a log, come down say he had done it, beaten Tashaka.

Well, he went up and up and he turned round and they were following him.

'What are you doing?'

'We are following you.'

'Why?'

'You will go halfway up and came down and say you've done it.'

'Why do you think that?'

'We know you.'

'Ah, ah, ah.'

Hiro went up and up, finally turned and they were gone. Oh! Hiro was delighted. He sat down on a log. Took out the dice, threw them.

'Ha ha ha, seven! Did it again. Ha ha ha!' Hiro was throwing the dice.

Out of the cave came Tashaka the god. He was enormous. He had orange hair and twisted teeth and looked way down at the little man throwing tiny, little white things with black dots.

Finally, Tashaka reached way down and touched the little man. 'What are these?'

'Dice, dice, dice.'

'Why do you call them dice, dice, dice?'

'I don't know, ha, ha, ha.'

'What do you do with them?'

'Make my living. I am the best in the world. Watch, I get seven every time. Oh, seven! Ha, ha, ha. Did it again. Ha, ha, ha.'

'You're the second best. I am the best.'

'Oh, no, no, no, you are the best at everything else. I am the best at the dice.'

'You shouldn't have said that. We are gonna have a contest. We'll throw the dice five times. Whoever gets the most sevens wins.'

'What's the prize?'

'The prize is your little head.'

'No, no, no, if I win?'

'If you win? I will give you my fan for one year.'

'Who goes first?'

'What do you mean, who goes first? I am the god. I go first.'

Tashaka took these tiny, little things in his huge hands. 'Six. Almost! Not enough. Hmm.'

He then threw a second time. He got a three. He threw them a third time. He got a four. 'That's it, three plus four equals seven.'

'You got to do it all at once.'

'I didn't know that.'

'You knew.'

'Yeah, I knew. Ha, ha, ha.' Tashaka got one seven in five times.

'My turn.' Hiro threw. 'Ha! Seven, did it again, ha, ha, ha.'

'We tied. We're equal.'

'Yeah, not for long.' Hiro threw them a second time. He got a seven. Threw them round his back, got a seven. Put them in his mouth, spat them out. Got another seven.

Tashaka growled.

'I won't do that again, ha ha ha.'

Hiro got five sevens and Tashaka trembled. 'Alright, I play fair. Here is my fan, one year! You bring it back in a year.'

'I bring it back in a year. I promise. Ha, ha, ha ha. What do you do with the fan?'

'Here, give it to me. I will show you. You see, you take the fan underneath your nose. Wag it like that. Your nose goes out and out and out. Look at my nose, ha, ha, ha. Wag it the other way, towards the nose. Nose comes back. Pretty good, eh?'

'Ahya! Pretty good, ha, ha, ha. See you in a year.'

Hiro took the fan and he started having a wonderful time wagging the fan, his nose went out and out and out, hit a rabbit. The rabbit bit his nose. Hoh, oh, oh, oh, oh. He wagged. The nose came all the way back with a little nibble in it. 'Oh, you bad rabbit!'

Still, he had a wonderful time. By the time he came to the

bottom of the mountain, all he wanted was to play the dice. He found his friends but his friends were all busy.

There was an enormous gathering on both sides of the street. Everyone was waiting for the princess. She was coming in a beautiful carriage. Everyone was cheering. She was a lovely young woman. She had the most delicate bone structure. She sat there on the top of the carriage, everyone cheering. Hiro was so short he couldn't see. Ah! Ah! So he climbed up a tree, out on a branch, right in the middle of the street.

The princess was coming when he waved. 'I am Hiro, the gambler, ha ha.'

She paid no attention because she didn't see him. He got furious. The carriage went underneath. He wagged his fan and the princess's nose went out and out and out and out. It was so long, finally it went straight along the street.

She was very quick of mind. She saw maybe ten samurai. 'You, you, you, you and you, pick up my nose!'

The ten of them lifted her nose. She came off the carriage and down they went, down the street holding her nose. They got to the end of the street but it was a right angle. They couldn't get it round.

She said, 'Forward a bit, forward, that's it. Back, forward.' She got them round the corners. Up they went to the castle. The gates were open.

These men came carrying that thing. The king said, 'What is it?'

'It's a nose.'

'Its not a nose.'

'I think it's a nose, your majesty.'

He saw his daughter was attached to this thing. She was brought into the great hall. Of course, it was the only place that would fit her. Poor young woman.

The king said, 'Anyone, anyone who can help my daughter get her nose back to normal can marry her. But, if you fail, or if you cause her any pain, it's your head!'

Nobody wanted to try but Hiro. He knew about it.

'Ha, ha, ha, marry the princess! Ha, ha, ha, ha.' He came up, knocked at the gate. That very morning the king was there, opened the door. 'What do you want?'

'I am Hiro the gambler, ha, ha, ha.'

'Stop dancing, you fool!'

'I will sort your daughter's nose.'

'Five minutes, Hiro! I've heard about you. Five minutes or it's your head.'

Hiro was escorted in. He was left alone with the princess. Her eyes went to the right. She saw Hiro, she fell in love with him. She said, 'I think you are very brave.'

'I think so too! Ha! Ha! Ha! Ha! Watch this.' He threw the dice. 'Ooh seven! Did it again! Ha! Ha! Ha!'

After four minutes she said, 'Please you will lose your head.'

'Alright,' said Hiro. He took the fan out, wagged it towards her. She lifted her hands and her nose was perfect again.

'I never realised what a beautiful thing a nose is. I think I am in love with you.'

'I think I am in love with me too. Ha! Ha! Ha!' He danced around.

The King came in. 'Stop dancing with yourself you fool. Alright, you marry her.'

There was a fine wedding ceremony. Hiro the gambler, he had the finest food, wonderful music. What a ceremony.

Oh, a year went by and Hiro thought, 'Ho, I should take the fan back but I won't, ha ha ha. Tashaka will never know!'

All year long the princess fell more and more in love with him and he fell more and more in love with himself, ha, ha, ha, ha. Well half a year after that went by, and he went away. All he wanted were the dusty streets and his dice and his friends, and he ran and ran and ran so the king could never find him.

One night he lay down and he was so hot that he went to sleep fanning himself. He was on his back, and as he fanned himself his nose was going up and up and up and up and up all night long, rising, rising. And that very night, Tashaka the god was making a bridge of the stars called the Milky Way. Everything was right except he needed one more little piece, and he looked down. Something was coming up and up and up. It was just right. It was Hiro's nose.

'That's what it is. It's Hiro's nose.'

He put it right in place and he tied it there. Ha! The Milky Way is finished. Then he pinched the nose. And Hiro, oh, he woke up and he saw his nose going up and up and up, so he began to fan furiously the other way, towards his face. But since his nose was tied to the Milky Way, his body rose and rose and rose. And finally Tashaka said, 'You didn't bring the fan back!'

'Ah, I forgot.'

'You didn't forget.'

'No, I didn't forget. Ah, ah, ah!' Hiro was wailing and wailing because he was tied to the bridge. 'Let me go!'

'No, I can't let you go. I need that little piece for the bridge. Give me the fan.'

Tashaka took the fan and went jumping off among the stars. And poor Hiro was left attached to the bridge of the Milky Way. He took out his dice, threw a seven.

'Ha! Did it again, did it again. Ha, ha, I couldn't be with a better person. Ha, ha, seven, did it again!'

And now they say if you get one of these wonderful telescopes and look away, away up into the heavens on a clear night you will see a tiny, little man throwing dice, way up there in the bridge of the Milky Way.

'Ha, seven, did it again, did it again!'

It is Hiro, the gambler.

The Poor Farmer

This traditional story is one that I found to be particularly popular with young people in schools.

Once in Ireland lived a poor farmer in a little cottage with his old blind mother, his crippled father and his childless, young wife.

Every night, however poor, they always put a wee saucer of milk and a bannock or oatcake out for the little people. But now the farmer was desperate, for he had only one tiny patch of potatoes left.

That morning he went out, and oh! He sniffed the air ... the reek and stench of decay. When he came to his field the little patch was rotted black, soft and black and stinking.

He sat down on a stone and wept.

Just then one of the wee folk, a little man, a fairy man appeared.

'Oh,' says he, 'you're sad, you're not happy.'

'No,' says the man, 'we've nothing now. Nothing to eat. Things are bad.'

'Maybe I could help,' says the wee man. 'I can give you one wish. Usually it would be three. But things are bad in fairyland just now so it's only the one! What will you wish for?'

'Oh, that's hard,' says the farmer. 'Can I go home and ask my wife and family their advice?'

'Good idea!' says the wee fellow. 'I'll be here tomorrow morning. I'll wait for you.'

So home went the farmer, told his family the story.

'Oh,' said his old, blind mother, 'my son, if only I could see I'd help about the place. Work morning till night and, oh, just to see the sweet morning sky again. Wish for my sight, son.'

'Husband, husband,' said his wife, 'you know how I'm longing for a bairn. If we just had a little one I'm sure our luck would turn. Oh, husband, wish for a baby.'

'Fools,' said the old father. 'What's the use of another mouth to feed and an old woman's sight when we're starving o' hunger. Gold, lad, wish for gold.'

Next day the young farmer returned, and there as promised sat the wee man.

'Well, did you decide?'

'Only one wish?' said the farmer.

'Sorry,' said the wee man, 'that's all I can manage, just the one.'

'Any wish?'

'Any wish,' said the wee man.

'Well,' said the farmer, 'I'd like my old blind mother to see our baby in a golden cradle.'

'Fine,' said the wee man, 'so it shall be!'

The Tax Collector at Jericho

This is an amended version of a story I wrote for BBC Scottish Schools Radio, subsequently published by Saint Andrew Press in the collection Tales to Tell II (1994). For the section on Mary Magdalene, I am indebted to an American minister who was visiting my wife at the time, Linda Bandelier. She had told me the minister had a wonderful additional piece about Zaccheus and Jesus. She had left the flat with this American minister to take him to the airport when I remembered this, opened the window and shouted down into the street, 'Zaccheus! Zaccheus!' So she returned from the airport with this wonderful section.

Small, small, that was the trouble, he had always been small. He had been a fine, plump little baby alright but then when all the other boys and girls in Jericho had sprung up and grown tall, he stayed small. He was the smallest boy in the neighbourhood and the others made fun of him; called him titchy, short legs or mouse. So he didn't have many friends. He didn't like people and they didn't like him. But if he was small, he was far from stupid. In fact, he was very clever and at an early age he decided that he was going to become rich, so rich that he could do what he liked. He would show these folk who called him names who was the biggest fool. He would have the largest house in the town and it would have its own swimming pool!

And he did become a rich man and owned nearly the largest house in the town and it had its own swimming pool. The only larger houses belonged to his Roman masters.

Rich, yes, he was rich, one of the richest men in Jericho. He was also one of the most detested men in Jericho because he made his money by collecting taxes from his fellow Jews for the hated Romans.

He was greedy and ruthless. He forced the Jews to pay three and four times the proper amount and pocketed the rest for himself. He had two 'protectors' as he called them, and if any poor Jew fell behind in his taxes these ugly characters, on some dark night, would visit him and break one of his bones to encourage him to pay. Or worse, they would threaten his wife and children. He had grown up to be a small and friendless little man.

He knocked at the door of a poor, little house. A pale, frightened woman shuffled to answer it. When she saw that it was the tax collector she burst into tears.

'You know my husband is blind. He has been begging in the market and on the streets but we have not enough money to buy food, not enough to live.'

He looked at her. 'You have one week to find the money. I will return in one week at this time. And if you do not pay me then it will be the worse for you.'

'But, sir …'

'One week!' He turned on his heels and was gone. In a narrow street he came to a house that he hated to visit. It was the house of a leper, a man with a skin disease.

The tax collector remembered the man's hollow eyes, the scabs and white, flaky skin on his face, and shuddered. He knocked and stood back. Once again he heard a shuffling and the door opened and the leper's wife stood there trembling when she saw who it was.

'Sir,' she said, 'please do not ask us for money. My husband cannot work; you know everyone avoids us. He has to carry the leper's bell to warn people of his disease.'

'Pay!' he said.

'Sir, we have not the money.'

'You have one week, or else!'

'But sir ...'

'One week!'

And once more he was gone, leaving the woman leaning against the door in tears. Now he turned and made his way to a prosperous part of the town, houses with high walls and gardens and locked gates, the mansions of the wealthy. Here he would surely get his money.

At the wrought iron gates of a fine mansion, he heard the sound of music. He could see beautiful fruit trees and a bubbling fountain; this was the mansion of Mary Magdalene who kept her house of pleasure for the Roman officers and centurions. She made a rich living.

He rang the great bell and soon the servant girl answered.

'Tell your mistress I've come to collect the tax.'

Without a word she ran off. Soon, not the servant girl but the mistress, Mary Magdalene, appeared in a bright, flowing, silken dress.

'Your taxes!' demanded the little man.

For answer, she came to the gate and spat in the face of the tax collector, hissing, 'Traitor!'

'And you,' growled the tax man, 'serving the Romans!'

'I take their money,' she said. 'You take the money of our people.' With that she turned and was gone.

'You will pay or else.'

A week passed and once more he stood at the door of the blind man's house. He knocked and heard a firm step walk to the door. It swung open and the man blinked at the light and said, 'Ah, you're the tax collector? I've been expecting you. Here is your money.' And he handed over a purse of coins. 'You'll find that is correct, sir,' he said. 'I counted it myself.'

The tax collector was speechless. He looked at the man.

'You can see!'

'Yes, I can see,' said the man, 'and I have earned this money. I am the happiest man on earth.'

'But how did this happen?' said the tax collector.

'The great teacher Jesus healed me. He took mud from the earth, spat upon it, laid it on my eyes and now I am cured. I can see. No one could be richer than I am now.'

The tax collector was amazed, and almost before he realized it, arrived at the house of the leper, where he hesitated and then knocked. Once more he heard firm steps, no shuffling, come to the door and there before him stood the leper. He sprang back as if whipped.

'Don't be afraid,' said the man. 'I've been expecting you. Here is your money. It's alright, I've counted it myself.'

The tax collector peered into the man's face. He couldn't believe it. Where once the eyes were hollow and glazed, now they were bright and warm. The skin of his face, once scabby and flaky, was fresh as a baby's.

'What happened?' he asked.

'I am cured!'

'Yes, but how?'

'The great healer Jesus healed me. There were ten of us and we were outside the town when Jesus came by with his friends and followers. I had heard of this great teacher and shouted out to him from a distance, "Jesus, master, take pity on us." He looked at us and said, "Go and let the priests examine you." No one could believe it. When we got to the temple and showed ourselves to the priests every one of us was cured, just as I am now.'

Dumbfounded, the little man turned to go to the Magdalene's house of pleasure. He would make her pay, or bring his protectors. She would not like them to destroy her beauty.

As he approached he was surprised at the silence, and when he came to the gate and rang the bell it was not the little servant girl but the mistress herself who answered. Gone was the silken dress. She wore black, modest black, opened the gate herself, came forward and said, 'Forgive me. I am sorry for what I did and said. Here is your money.'

'But what has happened?'

'My house is closed. The girls have gone. I met the great healer. I have changed my life. He has forgiven me. I am happy as I've never been.'

'But who is this man?'

'Some say he is a prophet and some that he is the Messiah, the Son of God himself, but I tell you he is the kindest and best man that ever lived and if God is like him, I believe in God. This man loves everyone.'

'Everyone,' thought the tax collector. 'He could not love me. No one loves me.' Out loud he said, 'And where can you find this man?'

'He will be in Jericho today,' said Mary Magdalene. 'He will walk down the main street I am sure, for already great crowds of people are gathered there waiting to see him and to hear him and to be healed by him. Listen, you can hear the crowds shouting. He is like an angel of God.'

The tax collector walked away slowly. He felt alone and small and ugly. He could see the hatred in the dark eyes of the people who looked at him. Yet, he found himself drawn to the main street, to where the great crowd was, to where Jesus was to pass. The murmuring grew like leaves scuttling in the wind.

'He is coming!' chanted the crowd.

The little man would be able to see nothing. He was small, that was the trouble. Even on tiptoe he would see nothing. So he ran ahead of the crowd and there by the roadside he saw a sycamore tree. It had branches that he could climb easily and they leaned out over the road. He scrambled up the tree to hide and wait. From here he could see this extraordinary man and no one would know he was there. As he waited, the crowds formed below him under the tree. The murmuring of the crowd came closer. Nearer and nearer came Jesus, speaking to the people, touching some, and he seemed to be like a man on fire.

And directly below the tree where the tax collector was hiding, Jesus stopped. He looked straight up into the branches, into the frightened eyes of the little man and said in a loud, clear voice, 'Zacchaeus, come down out of that tree!'

The crowd became silent as death. Little Zacchaeus clambered down and stood looking up at Jesus, the two of them surrounded by the huge crowd.

'Now the traitor will get his just desserts! Jesus will put him in his place.' Everyone waited.

'Tonight, Zacchaeus,' said Jesus clearly, 'I shall dine at your house.'

The eyes of Zacchaeus filled with tears. 'Sir, I will make everything ready.' And he ran off as fast as he could.

All of the people mumbled and grumbled and were bewildered. What was the great teacher doing, going to the house of a cheat, a swindler, a traitor to his own people, a ruthless and hated man?

But that night in the house of Zacchaeus was another miracle. The heart of the little tax collector was healed and he could see with new, loving eyes.

'Jesus, sir,' he said, 'I will give half my belongings to the poor and I will pay back four times more to anyone I have cheated.'

And Jesus said to the mumblers and grumblers, 'Don't you see, I came to save the lost, the swindlers and thieves and evil doers. This is a wonderful day. I would like you to rejoice with me.'

From that day on, Zacchaeus was a changed man. If he was still small, he had the biggest heart in Jericho, and no one who asked him for help was ever refused.

But one little secret he kept to himself. Every day just

before sunset he would disappear. Little Zacchaeus crept quietly away from the house taking a bucket. He filled it at the well and then, just before dark, thinking no one could see him, he made his way to the main street and there he watered the sycamore tree that he had climbed when he first saw the great healer.

Christmas Bell

This story I heard when I was a student at Emerson College, East Sussex. It was told by a young woman from Colombia, South America. In my telling of the story, I insert, where it seems appropriate, carols, the sound of the wind high in the tower and of course the sound of the Christmas bell, which I replicate by using a singing bowl.

> *Your mild and gentle eyes proclaim*
> *The loving heart from which you came*
> *A tiny, tender, helpless babe*
> *With boundless gifts of grace*
> *Alleluia, alleluia, alleluia, alleluia*

(Christ Child's Lullaby, traditional Gaelic carol)

A long, long time ago, in a far, far country, there was a great cathedral. This cathedral rose magnificently on a hill in the middle of the town. The tower reached high into the sky, almost looking into the hazy clouds. In that land, there was a mysterious legend about it.

Now it was said that in this tower there hung a Christmas bell. Nobody in living memory had ever heard the sound of this bell. But still people gathered in the cathedral to offer their gifts to the baby Jesus on Christmas Eve. For the legend said that, when someone offered a gift that pleased the heart of Jesus, the bell in this great tower would start to ring by itself.

'I don't believe it. It's impossible for the bell to ring by itself.'

'Why not? The tower is so near to heaven that I think the angels could come down out of the clouds to ring the bell.'

'Hmm,' said an old man, 'the bell doesn't ring because no one has ever offered a gift that pleases the heart of the baby Jesus. If we offer a real gift, it will ring.'

Each year people brought gifts. Each year the gifts were more rich, more lavish, more extravagant because people wanted to boast that their gift had pleased the heart of the baby Jesus, had rung the Christmas bell. They brought their gifts not out of sincerity but out of vanity.

Every year on Christmas Eve the people gathered in the cathedral that was shining with stars, a thousand candles, the air filled with the sweet scent of incense, the wonderful music of the organ and the singing of the choir. The altar was piled with a mountain of gifts, and as the people brought their gifts they listened and listened, but they heard only the sighing of the wind high in the tower.

In a village further away from the town, there lived a boy called Pedro and his little brother. They didn't know anything about the bell. But they had heard about the wonderful Christmas Eve in a beautiful cathedral.

'Let's go to town this Christmas Eve and visit that cathedral!' Many times since summer, Pedro had said this to his little brother.

'It must be very beautiful. Just imagine! The beautiful sound of the organ and the thousands of candles.' When Pedro talked to his brother his eyes shone bright as candles.

Summer had passed, autumn had passed and now winter had come. It was the day they had long been waiting for. The snow was falling and it was cold. But their hearts were filled with the thought of candles and joyful music. How excited they were as they walked through the snow. Pedro's hand was in his pocket. He was holding a silver coin which he had earned helping his neighbours.

The snow was falling ever harder and harder, covering the ground. When Pedro and his brother arrived at the big gate of the town, it was already dark. And Pedro saw a bundle lying in the snow.

'What's this?' he cried. When he walked closer, he saw it was a poor woman dressed in rags. She had fainted and was lying there. Pedro touched her forehead. It was burning with a high fever.

'If we leave her here she is sure to die,' said Pedro. 'I will stay here and look after her. You go to the cathedral alone and offer this coin instead of me.' He took the silver coin out of his pocket and let his brother hold it firmly, and he said, 'Watch everything carefully and pray to Jesus for both of us and tell me everything that you see.'

So grasping the small silver coin in his hand, the little brother ran off through the snow as fast as he could. Pedro watched him grow smaller and smaller as the little figure hurried up the hill to the cathedral. Pedro began to brush the snow from the coat of the woman and stroke her back gently, but the tears ran down his face and dropped into the snow because now he knew he would not see Christmas in the great cathedral.

'But it is right for me to be here,' he thought, 'or this woman would have died.' So he continued to stroke her back.

The cathedral was filled with the solemn music of the organ and sweet singing of the choir. The people were gathering in their finest and brightest and richest clothes. One by one they began to take their gifts to the altar. They brought valuable jewels, boxes full of gold coins, rare ornaments, fine silks. Each one hoped that the bell would ring for them. They listened but heard only the sound of the cold wind.

At last the king himself came before the altar. He thought,

'Tonight my gift will ring the Christmas Bell.' And he took the crown from his head and laid it there on the altar. As he did so, everybody in the cathedral gasped.

'The King has given his crown.'

'Now surely the bell will ring.'

'Yes, yes, yes, because such a thing has never happened before and will never happen again.'

'Yes, the bell will ring!'

The people whispered. Then they waited ... and listened ... but they heard only the sound of the wind high in the tower.

'Oh,' said the people, 'this legend was never true.'

'For surely the crown of a king would ring the bell!'

'Yes, it was only a story.'

'The bell has never rung.'

'We have been fools to believe it.'

The cathedral was full of the noise of the chattering people. Suddenly, the priest raised his hand for silence and a great hush fell upon the people. Once more they listened.

Then came the sound. From the high sky came the beautiful, beautiful sound of the bell. So pure and majestic that it poured deep and deep into the hearts of the people. It was as if an enchantment had fallen upon them.

They gazed towards the altar. Who could have given a gift to ring the bell? What gift could be better than the crown of the king?

There stood Pedro's little brother. 'Why are all these people looking at me?' he wondered. Among all the rich gifts on the altar, one little, silver coin shone out like a star.

And in the little hovel where Pedro had taken the old woman she lay on a bed of straw. She opened her eyes, looked into the face of Pedro and smiled. She said, 'Someone has given a gift that has pleased the heart of the baby Jesus, a gift that has rung the Christmas bell.'

The Caged Bird

I was captivated when I heard Roi Gal-or tell this story at Emerson College, East Sussex. It is made the more intriguing by its ambiguous conclusion. When I tell this story, I adopt a French persona and accent, which I think makes it more effective.

Pierre Le Grand. Pierre Le Grand – a good name, I can say, yes, yes! I look around me – my office, everything is, as the English would say, 'grand'. Pierre Le Grand. I have everything, but … I am not happy. Something is wrong. Look at this office. All these people. They are well paid, the best paid in all of Paris. Look at their comfortable seats and the long breaks I give them. Ivory telephones and the very latest in technology but despite that, I am not happy. What is wrong, Pierre?

I know what is wrong. I should have a holiday! I'll take my beautiful open top Mercedes, I'll go for a drive in the country and see what happens. Goodbye office! I will take a little break.

Ah! Look at this. The open road, the birds singing in the trees, all this greenery! I haven't seen so much green for years it seems. You are starved Pierre, starved! Look at this little village, a lovely, little village. Ahh! And look at that little lane there. The people have looked after it well – the trees, the garden. I'll leave the car here and take a little walk up there.

Oh, look at that old couple.

'Bonjour monsieur, madame. Oh, but what a beautiful bird you have there. What a beautiful bird! So beautiful. Does the bird sing?'

'Ah oui, monsieur, she has got the most beautiful voice in the whole countryside. Listen, listen!'

'Oh! That is a song to enchant the heart; a beautiful, beautiful, singing bird. How much would you wish for that bird?'

'Oh, monsieur, that bird, that goldfinch, is not for sale. My wife Marie and me, we prize that bird, it is our most precious possession.'

'I don't think you quite understand. You just name the price. You could have a holiday for the rest of your life. The money I could give you; I have bountiful money, as they say in the English, bountiful money.'

'Monsieur, I have no doubt you are very rich but, non, it is not for sale.'

'Ah, very well, I wish you both very good luck.'

Well, I'll go into the village. What is this? It is a bird. It looks like a goldfinch.

'Monsieur, that goldfinch there, in the cage outside your shop, how much is it?'

'Ah, you can have both the bird and the cage for twenty-five francs.'

'What? Is that bird alright?'

'Oui monsieur, it is perfectly alright, but it does not sing.'

'Ah, it does not sing.' I am a businessman. I have business-like thoughts all the time. 'I'll take the bird and the cage. Twenty-five francs?'

'Thank you very much, monsieur.'

Now I'll wait until it's getting dark and then when the old couple have retired to bed, I'll take this bird and just make a little exchange, that's what I'll do.

Ah, it is covered with a cloth. I think the old couple must

be asleep. I'll just put my bird in that cage and I take the singing bird with me. And what a wonder it will be when I take it back to my office in Paris!

'Today I have a surprise for all of you, a wonderful surprise. A little bird. I take off the cover, and listen to the beautiful song!' So beautiful. The atmosphere in the office is transformed.

Ah, we've had this bird now three beautiful weeks, but I am haunted, haunted by the old couple. This bird was their prized possession, and I have everything. I'll take it back!

Once more, look at the countryside. What a beautiful drive, the birds singing in the trees. Once more the lovely, little village. And here is the lane where the old couple live. I'll leave the car here and I'll leave the bird here, and go up and see how they are first of all.

'Good evening, monsieur.'

'Good evening, sir.'

'But where is your wife, Marie?'

'Ah, when Marie discovered our bird would not sing any more, she lost her heart. And when she lost her heart, she died.'

'Oh, I am very sorry, so sorry to hear that.'

Now what will I do?

What would you do?

Fat Murray

This chilling story I heard from a feisty, seasoned storyteller, Zoe, in Sydney. She said it never failed with classes of adrenalized teenage boys. By its first sentences she had their attention, and the last paragraph drew a ready discussion of how they considered the tale should continue. Like Zoe, I found this an ideal tale to begin with for a group of adolescents; it promoted animated discussion about what the audience thought happened and what they would have done; everything from shoot one or the other or both to throw away the gun and leave. A winner as a beginner!

A life sentence.
Thirteen years for a murder I didn't commit.
I waited, counted the days, every single day.
And made a vow. I knew what I was going to do.
I'd been the model prisoner, never complained
about the food, about the screws,
avoided trouble with other prisoners,
kept my nose clean.

The last days, the last hours, were the worst –
the others trying to trip me up. And the screws.
But I kept quiet, silent, cool.
And finally the day came –
the day of my release.

I fetched my clothes
and the small amount of money that I'd gone in with.
Walked out through the gates, a free man.
Bought something to eat ... and a gun.
Then set off for the house of Fat Murray.

I came up the drive. Strangely quiet.
Usually there was some sign of the girls,
always some sound, music or chatter.
Murray always had something going on, but no, not a sound.
Rang the bell, felt for the gun in my pocket.
I could not wait to see Murray.

The door opened, not as I was expecting by a young woman,
but by an older woman, small, grey hair, bright eyes.
'I've come to see Murray. Is he in?'
'You want to see Murray?'
'Yes.'
'You can see Murray. Just go through. He's in his room.'

Strangely empty, the place seemed eerily quiet.
Always some music for the girls, always bustle,
signs of a party.

'Go through, you can see Murray.'
She pointed to the big, old, wood panelled door I remembered
so clearly.
Murray's room!
'Don't bother to knock,' she said, 'just go in.'

I felt a tingle, checked the gun.
I opened the door. The light was dim. Curtains drawn.
And there he was.
Hands manacled above him. Feet manacled to the floor.
A gaunt figure in a hot, sultry room.

This had been Fat Murray – great belly,
fat cheeks, hanging chins, blubbery lips ... all gone.
And this skeleton with a covering of skin, hanging there.
Eyes glazed, gazing emptily, hollow eyes ...
a broken figure.

It was Murray – a shell of Murray.
He looked straight at me, eyes pleading. Did he recognise me?
I heard a sound, turned around.

The little lady stood there.
'You wanted to see Murray. This is Murray!
You are the young man they put away for Shelley's murder.'
'Yes, but I didn't do it. Murray did it.'
'Yes,' said the little lady, 'I know. I'm Shelley's mother.
You see, I came to see Murray, Fat Murray.
I said to him, "Look, these young girls,
they attract the customers,
but they don't keep your place tidy, tidy as it deserves to be.
I need a job as a housekeeper. Cheap."

And I kept the place immaculate, and waited my time.
Then one night, Fat Murray, drunk. It was easy.
I had it planned. Knocked him cold.
That's nearly thirteen years ago.'

'I came to kill him.'
'Oh no, oh no,' said the little lady.
'I don't want Murray dead. I keep him alive, see.
Feed him just enough ... just enough to keep him alive.'

I had the gun out.
What to do?

Goodbye

In 1987 I spent six weeks in Tantur Ecumenical Institute in Jerusalem on a hill near Bethlehem. Newly married, I was visiting my second wife, American Methodist Minister, Linda Bandelier. I was one day taking a trip to Masada, the last outpost of Jewish resistance against the Romans in 73 A.D. It is an almost impregnable high rock buttress overlooking the Dead Sea. This fortress, I was visiting with a party of mainly American pilgrims. On the bus there, I was sitting beside an elderly American woman, Mary Ingenthorn. I was holding her hand. 'David,' she said, 'no one but my husband has held my hand since we were married, but I don't think he'll mind.'

As we sat there, she said, 'I would like to tell you a dream I had.'

At the end of her telling, I said, 'Mary, that should be written in a book or broadcast on the radio.'

'Well, David, you do that.'

I did. It became the last story in my book, Tales to Tell II, *Saint Andrew Press, 1994, and a BBC Radio broadcast I produced for children leaving primary school to attend secondary.*

Subsequently, when I was in the States, I visited Mary and her husband and presented them with the book and tape recording of the broadcast.

To have good fruit you must have a good, healthy tree; if you have a poor tree, you will have bad fruit. A tree is known by the kind of fruit it bears.
(Matthew 12:33 GNT)

Our story begins during a leafy summer not very long ago. School was over for the day in the little Scottish village of Kilbracken. Three pals walked down the village street. For once they were all quiet – they were all thinking and they were all hiding tears. Who would have believed that, today of all days, they would have lumps in their throats, far less tears in their eyes.

'Especially me,' thought Alan. He kept his curly, dark head down as he looked at his misty feet, hoping that Caroline and Wendy wouldn't notice. But Caroline and Wendy were busy with their own thoughts.

This was the day they had all looked forward to. They had talked about it for weeks. The last day of term, their very last day at primary school, the end of Primary 7 – freedom!

'And here I am,' thought Caroline, 'bubbling like a kid in Primary 1 on my first day of school!'

'Let's go and climb our tree,' suggested Wendy. Without a word the others followed her along the path by the river to their special meeting place.

They were all good climbers and scrambled up into their own perch on a branch of their favourite tree. From there they looked down into the pool where Caroline and Alan had done a life-saving job on Wendy's kitten when it fell in. In fact, that was how they all came to be friends in the first place. But that is another story. For now, they all looked down into the pool and thought about the future. And they were thinking about the future not just because it was the last day of term, but because of the words that were still ringing like fading bells in their ears.

At the end of the service that morning, the headmistress had dismissed every class in the school except Primary 7. They were left, one little class standing in the big hall. The headmistress, Mrs Campbell, said, 'I have a surprise for you all. Follow me.'

And she led the class out of the school, down the street and into the only hotel in the village. She led them upstairs and stood before a door.

'Now in you go,' she said.

There in front of them was a table with names written on cards in front of each place, the names of every child in the class. The names were neatly written by hand and they at once recognised the handwriting. They had all copied that writing when they were in Primary 1. It was the careful handwriting of Mrs Campbell.

'Eat as much as you like,' she told them.

It was indeed a feast, a wonderful feast.

But it was not the food that brought tears to the eyes of Alan, Caroline and Wendy. No, it was Mrs Campbell's story. She could always tell a good story.

After they had eaten as much as they possibly could, and in some cases a little more, Mrs Campbell had said to them, 'Primary 7, I want to give you all something to take away with you. I am going to give you one last story from me. A story is better than any toy because you can keep it forever. It will never break or wear out and you can give it away and still have it. The more you give it away the better it gets. This story is especially for you. Perhaps you won't know this, but today is a special occasion for me as well as you. You are my very last Primary 7. Like you, I am leaving, so today is goodbye. That is why we are having this feast together.

Well, I lay in bed last night and wondered what I could say to you. While I was thinking, I fell asleep and when I was sleeping, I had a dream. I am going to tell you my dream.

In my dream I became as light as air. I was a space traveller. My mission was to visit many planets and find out what their customs were. Of all the planets I observed, one memory is more vivid than all the rest; it is of my brief visit to the little planet of Womantu.

I landed at the space platform and asked directions from one of the local people. There was something very beautiful and strangely familiar about his face, but at the time I couldn't make out what it was. Then I made my way on foot to the centre of the town. It seemed like the whole town was gathered together for some kind of ceremony. All the townspeople were clad in long cloaks of hand-woven cloth. The cloaks were plain grey and all similar in design. I asked a friendly, young man beside me whose face was also strangely familiar, the reason for the gathering.

He told me, 'It is called the Transformation of the Cloak, a ceremony of goodbye.' Then I saw that it was a kind of funeral, because there, laid out upon the altar of stone, was the body of a very old man. He too, wore a plain cloak. Beneath it I realised that his clothes were shabby and threadbare. Clearly this man had been very poor. The lad told me the old man had been a carpenter.

I then asked the lad about the cloaks. He said that every inhabitant of that place was given a cloak the moment they were born. The cloaks grew as they grew. The cloaks were always clean and had a beautiful, light scent like wild summer flowers.

As I was talking to this young man, I became aware of a growing murmuring amongst the crowd ... an excited murmuring. I turned in the direction of the old man on the altar. And, Primary 7, an amazing sight met my eyes. For, as if sewn by invisible hands, beautiful embroidery began to appear and shimmer on the cloak of the old man. Everyone watched in silence as marvellous patterns and designs began to appear in colours of red and blue and gold, beautiful colours and patterns, until it seemed that the face of the old man shone, even in death.

Well, every square of the cloak shimmered like silk and bore marvellous embroidery. I was completely astonished and, as you can imagine, quite curious, so I asked the lad beside me if this always happened. The youth laughed. 'Oh no, no, no,' he said. 'Sometimes the cloak falls into tatters; sometimes little patches of embroidery appear; and sometimes it's just a mess. This is a very ancient ceremony. The wise folk say that the colours and embroidery tell the story of the dead person's life. Look there.' He pointed at the cloak of the dead man. 'Red and blue and gold. They say red is for courage and blue for honesty and gold for love. You see, this old man has lived a very good life.'

Just then, we were interrupted by a great clapping and chanting. The people were applauding the old man's cloak as if it were the end of a great theatre performance. Some were even cheering and chanting, 'God be with you! God be with you! Goodbye! Goodbye!' But then it became, 'Goodbye and hello! Goodbye and hello!'

I asked the lad why. He looked at me as though I were simple-minded and said, 'Don't you know that every goodbye is also a hello?'

Suddenly I saw the sun going down over a distant hill, and when I looked round again the young man was gone, and the crowd, everything. My dream was gone too. The last thing I heard was the sun whispering, 'Hello.' I awoke and there was the sun, a red glow shining out of a blue sky turning the walls of my room gold.

And so, Primary 7, I knew that this story was for you, it is my goodbye to you. I have seen you all from the time you arrived in Primary 1, with your shining faces, clean and new. Seven years ago it was, more than half your lives ago! And now you have most of your lives ahead of you ... as I have most of my life behind me.

Well, there is one thing I didn't tell you about my dream. The reason I found the faces of the townspeople of Womantu familiar was that the faces were your faces, Primary 7, your faces. You are all stories waiting to be told.'

Mrs Campbell got up out of her chair and walked over to the door, whispering, 'Remember, Primary 7, red and blue and best of all gold. Goodbye, my children, goodbye Primary 7. God be with you ... God be with you all!'

The Flying Horse of Earthdom

This is a wonder tale by Duncan Williamson, told to him by a cousin of his father, also named Duncan Williamson. Duncan told me that a story was a gift that was valuable only if you passed it on. I had always liked this story and, after a particularly lengthy falling out between us, Duncan sat me down one day and said, 'David, you've always wanted to know this story, and so I'm going to tell it to you so that you can pass it on, and it will be a sign that you and me will never, never have another disagreement.' Of course, this was not to be true, but I have told and valued this story as one of my favourites.

The story begins a long time ago. Back into history, there once lived a great king. Where his kingdom was, the story doesn't tell, but he was loved by some, hated by some, worshipped by some.

He lived with his queen in a great, old stone palace. Now the love of his heart was his two little twin sons. He loved the boys dearly; he couldn't get enough time for them. Sometimes he'd give up hunting, he would give up battle; he loved these sons dearly. The queen was loved and respected by everyone and her dearest friend, apart from the king, was the old hen woman who lived not far from the palace in a little cottage and kept hens by the seaside. They had spent many happy times together and the longing of the queen's heart, she would tell her friend, was to have a baby girl.

She knew how much the king loved their sons. She, of course, too loved their sons, but she wanted a little girl and she kept telling the king this. The king would say, 'Girls, girls, girls, all we hear about is girls, girls, girls. You should be happy with what you've got.'

But after a few visits to her friend the hen-wife, and what passed between her and the hen-wife, the queen became pregnant. When she told the king, the king was delighted. 'Maybe another son,' he said. The king loved his sons.

The months flew by very quickly and, lo and behold, the queen gave birth and to the king's delight, another son. The king was overjoyed; he was called to the queen's bedside a couple of hours later and she passed the little, wrinkly, newborn baby to the king and said, 'You've got what you wished for.'

And the king took one look and thrust the baby into the queen's bosom. It was a bonnie little boy, but he had a hump on his back and his spine was bent. The king was so upset he said, 'I didn't father that. That doesn't belong to me!'

She said, 'Of course, my king, it is your son.'

'I can't have that,' he said, 'to grow up and disgrace me.'

'But,' the queen said, 'it's your son, my king, it's your son.'

'That's no son of mine,' he said. 'My son will grow up strong and tall like me. That has to go out of our sight.'

The queen began to cry.

The king said, 'There is no option. It has to go.'

'But,' the queen said, 'what are you going to do with him?'

He said, 'Leave it to me. Tomorrow we will have a mock burial. It has died.' And he ordered the servant to take the baby away.

The queen's heart was nearly broken with sorrow, but the next day there was a mock funeral and many people gathered and buried the little coffin in the graveyard, the cemetery behind the palace.

But secretly the king had the baby in another room with

an old woman who respected the king. He called on one of his huntsmen late in the evening and told the huntsman, 'Huntsman, I want you to take this baby of mine. Take it out to the forest as far as you can. Destroy it and bring me back evidence.'

The huntsman didn't know what to do because he was a father himself and had children of his own, but he could not go against the king's orders. So late that night the king bundled up the little baby and passed it to the huntsman and he rode off, but before going off into the forest he called at the house of the old hen-wife. He told the hen-wife the story. He was nearly crying.

'I don't know what to do,' he said. 'I can't go against my king, and I'm a family man and have children of my own. What can I do with this little baby?'

The hen-wife gave him something to eat and drink and she said, 'Don't worry, just a moment.' She kept a goat or two and she fetched a big bottle of goat's milk with a little teat. She wrapped it in a little piece of flannel and she said, 'Take this with you into the forest, till you come to a great oak tree. Sit under the oak tree, then just wait. If the baby cries, feed him on this.' She bade the huntsman goodbye and off he rode into the forest.

He rode for some time with the directions the old hen-wife had given him until he came to the old oak tree and there he sat. He sat there and his heart was breaking with sorrow.

'Who could destroy a little baby like this?' He held him in his arms, he looked at the little creature. Yes, he had a hump on his back but he was a little child! He thought of the sadness of the queen but he could not go against the orders of the king.

He sat till dawn was breaking when he heard the clop, clop, clop of feet, like the feet of a horse. He stared down the old pathway and sure enough coming towards him was an old hunchbacked man with a long, white beard, dressed in goatskin. He had a donkey that was carrying many little packs. The old man looked at the huntsman and said, 'You look kind of sad, stranger.'

The huntsman spoke. 'Yes, I'm very sad. It's a terrible thing I have put upon me.'

'What has been put upon you?' asked the old man.

'I'm here to destroy this little one.'

The old man left the donkey. The donkey just stood with hanging head while the old man lifted the baby, looked at it, and the most amazing thing! When he pulled back the covering that the old woman had wrapped the baby in, the baby looked up and smiled at the old man, though it was only a few days old.

And the old hunchback said, 'Never worry my friend, you'll have no trouble.' He reached into his pack and brought out a rabbit. He said, 'Give me your sword,' and he passed it through the rabbit two or three times.

He put his hand in the purse he carried by his side and gave the huntsman two gold coins. 'As far as you are concerned,' he said, 'the baby is gone.'

It was a very relieved huntsman who climbed on his horse with blood on his sword and rode back to the palace and presented himself before the king. The king was overjoyed.

'There'll be no more of him,' he said.

The old hunchback took the little baby up beside him in the saddle on the donkey and he travelled on through the forest, winding his way between the trees and bushes until he came to a great cliff in the hillside. Through a secret passage among the trees the hunchback passed. The sun was just rising as he padded into the most beautiful valley anyone had ever seen.

It was full of little cabins like a market garden and when the people saw them coming, they all came running towards them, clapping their hands; some with club foot, some missing a leg, some hunchbacked, some blind, some deaf, some not able to speak. There was not a person in the whole crowd – and there must have been fifty or sixty, young, old, children too – who was not disabled in some way. They all came, laughing and happy, around the hunchback. From his pack he gave things to them all and they went on their way.

Through this valley of gardens and flowers went the hunchback. It was the most beautiful place you could find. The hunchback went to one of the largest cabins, gave the donkey to a young lad who put it in a little stable by the cabin's side and there sitting, rocking herself in an old wooden chair, was an old woman.

He came up with the baby in his arms and she said, 'Oh, you've brought me something, another one.'

'Yes, my dear,' he said, 'I've brought you another one, but this one is very special.'

She said, 'They're all very special to me.'

In this beautiful, green valley the old hunchback and the old woman were as kings and queens, caring for the people of the secret, hidden valley of Earthdom. Only the hunchback knew the entrance to this place; no one else knew they existed, all these people. Whenever he found someone the world did not want, the hunchback brought them to this secret valley and there they stayed, amongst friends, happy to the end of their days.

In this beautiful, hidden, secret valley of Earthdom, the years flew by and the young, humble prince, not knowing who he was, grew up with the old hunchback and the old woman. To him they were as a father and a mother. The old hunchback taught him the ways of the moors and the rivers, taught him how to fire an arrow, taught him how to wield a sword. Many happy and wonderful times they had together at fencing and archery and ranging the secret valley, and he took him riding. Aside from the old donkey there was only one horse in the whole valley, an old white horse. The creature looked ancient in years but it could be swift enough.

So there he lived content and well till he was eighteen years of age. He had grown, despite the hunch, into a tall and muscular, strong and handsome young man. The old man and the old woman loved him like a son. And everyone in the valley was his friend.

Then one morning the old hunchback called the young man before him. 'My son,' he said, 'I have a task for you.'

'Yes, father, what do you want me to do for you?'

'Far from here,' said the old hunchback, 'is the city of the king and the palace of the king. In that place there is to be a great tournament to celebrate the twenty-first birthday of the king's two twin sons. My son, I wish you to compete in three contests: the archery you are so skilled in, the sword fencing and the best – the horse racing. I want you to do your best for me.'

'I would love to do that for you,' said the young man, 'but I have never been outside this valley. How will I find my way?'

'I will show you the way!' said the old man.

'But, father,' said he, 'what shall I do for a horse?'

'We have a horse, the swiftest in the land.'

The young hunchback was a little dubious. The old mare had never gone beyond a lazy trot with him.

'Come with me, my son, climb up!'

So the young man swung up, no saddle, barely a bridle, and the old hunchback swung up behind him.

'Now, my son,' he said, 'let's do some speed.'

The old hunchback reached over the young boy's shoulders, pressed his two thumbs into the horse's neck and said, 'Faster, boy, faster!'

Suddenly the wind was in their faces as they sped over the ground.

'Where is all this speed coming from?' said the young man.

'There is yet more,' said the old hunchback. And again he reached over, pressed his two thumbs into the horse's shoulders and said, 'Up and away.' And all in a moment a pair of beautiful, silver wings unfolded and they lifted and soared from the ground. Like a wonderful bird they floated and circled round the valley. The young man gazed down in amazement and delight and they glided gracefully back to earth. The wings folded and were gone.

The old man smiled. 'Tomorrow you shall travel to the palace of the king. And my son, if ever you are in trouble or danger, you know what to do; press your thumbs into the horse's shoulders and say, "Up and away!"'

So next morning he led the young hunchback through the cliff passage, who went on his way saying farewell to the only one he'd ever known as his father. He travelled for a day and a night and a day and a night, and on the third day he heard music, saw the flags waving from the rampart of the palace. He had never seen anything like this before in his life so he rode through the gate, the entrance to the palace where the great tournament was to be held.

He was instantly stopped by two guards who asked, 'Where do you think you are going?'

He said, 'I have come a long way to compete in the great feats.'

They looked at the strange young man and exchanged amused glances.

'Oh, anyone is free to enter. What great feats are you for?'
'The swordsmanship,' said he and they chuckled.
'The archery,' said he and they laughed out loud.
'And most important, the horse racing.' They doubled up.
'On your way. Good luck!'

Followed by their howls of laughter, he entered the city. He found something to eat, something to drink and somewhere to sleep. Next morning was the great day. He competed in the archery until three competitors remained. Two strong, handsome young men, the king's twin sons, and himself. From the royal balcony the king and queen saw their two sons put to shame by the skill of this stranger.

In the sword fencing it was the same. The stranger out-pointed, out- manoeuvred, out-fought the king's sons and put them to shame. The king was red with fury. And then the greatest event, the horse race round the wall of the city with the finest horses in the land.

From the royal balcony the queen dropped a golden ball. They were off, thundering through the city gates. All round the walls the crowd cheered and roared, then fell strangely silent. And then, like a whirlwind clear of the field, bursting through the gates past the winning post, came the old white mare and its rider, the young stranger. The king's sons followed, and then the best horses in the land.

The king roared to the guards, 'Bring that man before me.'

At once the guards and soldiers ran towards the young hunchback. Afraid he was being attacked, he pressed his thumbs to the horse's shoulders. 'Faster boy, faster! Up and away!' And the two silver wings unfolded. The horse rose, a graceful wonder, flew out over the city and disappeared above the distant forest.

The king fell into a fury of obsession. He questioned everyone. No one could tell of this young man. He sent couriers and messengers over the land seeking the flying horse and the young man who rode it, but to no avail. One evening, as the queen saw him sitting brooding by the fire, she said, 'Maybe I could help you.'

'You could help me! You could help me? When all my couriers, army and advisers riding the country round can't find this man. You could help?'

She said quietly, 'Maybe my friend the hen-wife could help.'

He calmed down. 'Do you think so?'

'Ask her.'

At once the king set out to where she lived. The old, wise hen-wife knew the king. She treated him as she would anyone in the world, and she already knew he was coming.

'I know you are obsessed in your mind,' said she. 'You are looking for the flying horse of Earthdom.'

'The flying horse of where?'

'The flying horse of Earthdom.'

'I have never heard of such a place,' said he.

'In your kingdom there is a secret valley, the hidden valley of Earthdom. And that is what you will need to find.'

'Just tell me. I will go myself!'

'Do as I say and you may find it. Take off your coat.'

'Take off ...' But the king removed his coat. Inside the shoulder the old woman sewed a cushion.

'Now put on your coat!'

When the King put on his coat there was a hump on his back.

'Why this?' said he.

'Without this,' said she, 'you will never find the way. Without this you will never find the hidden valley of Earthdom. You will wander in the forest, maybe for days, until you come to a great, old oak tree. Wait there until someone comes for you, even though you are starving of hunger.' She made him a little bundle of food for the journey.

The king made his way into the forest and wandered for days, lost, but came to a track and at last to the great, old oak tree. There he sat all night long till the chirping of the birds ceased and the forest was silent. He woke cold and hungry as the first light of day wakened the birds. Then he heard the clop, clop of hooves. And there, leading a donkey, was the old hunchback.

'Good day, stranger. You seem troubled. Are you in pain?' asked the hunchback.

'Just the pains of hunger and thirst,' said the king.

'We can cure that. Follow me.'

So through the forest the king followed the old hunchback and his donkey through winding ways and secret trails till they came to a great cliff. Concealed among the bushes was the secret passage.

Out they came into the most beautiful valley the king had ever seen: flowers, fruit trees, beautiful gardens, the air scented and fragrant. And from neat, little cabins people came clapping and laughing and surrounded the hunchback: some crippled, some blind, not one without a disability. The king was bewildered and startled.

'Who are these people?' he asked.

'Don't be troubled, they will not harm you. They are my friends, my people.'

He led the king to a fine wood cabin and sitting outside was a young man. 'Son, I have brought someone to meet you.'

The young hunchback stood up, greeted the king who at once knew that this was the person he sought. So together they sat, and after some food and drink the young man and the king talked long into the night. In the morning, they walked round the gardens and everyone greeted the young man with smiles and happiness. The king was amazed. He did not know such a place existed.

At length he asked, 'How do you pass your time when you are not tending these beautiful gardens?'

'I practice my archery!'

'Archery,' said the king, 'ah, that was once the love of my heart. But, well, with my back ...'

'Stay awhile,' said the young man. So the king stayed.

Back in the palace, the queen and court wondered what had happened to the king. But when the queen visited her friend, the old hen-wife, she said, 'Don't fret. He is in good hands and will return.'

So the queen was content.

Now the king stayed there in that beautiful valley for many days, admiring the gardens, talking to the people, getting to know the old hunchback and the young man. He learned once more the skills of archery and of left-handed swordsmanship. The young hunchback was his teacher, and he taught him well. The king became quite expert because, of course, he had practiced these skills all his life.

One day he said to the young hunchback, 'You have a wonderful place here.'

'Well,' he said, 'this is my home.'

'How long have you lived here?'

'I've lived here all my life. I can't remember anything else.'

The king said, 'I wonder what this place would look like from up amongst the clouds?'

And the young hunchback said, 'Would you like to see it from above?'

'Oh,' said the king, 'it's impossible. I'd need to be a bird to fly up there.'

'Come with me then,' said the young hunchback, and he led him to the stable beside the little cabin they lived in. He took out the old, white horse, put a bridle on his head and said to the king, 'Climb up on his back!'

So the king climbed up. The young hunchback jumped up before him and they rode for a bit, rode for a bit and another bit and then he pressed his thumbs into the horse's shoulders and the king heard the words plainly: 'Up and away.' And just like that out came the silver wings once more and the king gazed down. Not too high they were, just above the valley, and all the people were staring up at them and the king gave them a little wave, and round and round they went and landed once again near the little cabin.

There stood the old hunchback. He turned to the king and he said, 'You can come down now, Your Majesty. You've found what you came for. Take off that coat!'

The king dismounted and took off the coat, and there he stood, straight and tall.

'Now,' said the old hunchback, 'you've found what you want.'

The king said, 'Yes, I came looking for a young man who

put my whole palace to shame and now I have found him.'

And the old man turned round to the young hunchback and said, 'My son, do you know who this is? This is the king, this is your king ... not only your king but also your father.'

'My father?' said the young hunchback, 'but you are my father.'

'No, my son, I'm not your father. This is your father, the father who sent you to be killed in the forest with a huntsman. He was ashamed of you because of the hump on your back.'

The king was put to shame. He stepped towards the young man and the young man stepped away from him. 'Son,' he said, 'son, you are my son.'

'Of course,' said the old hunchback. 'He is your son. He is the son you sent to the forest to be killed because you were ashamed of him. And all the people around us here, are you ashamed of them? Are they not your subjects? Not your subjects because they have a hump on their back or a club foot or want an eye or cannot speak or cannot walk or cannot hear. Are you ashamed of them?'

The king's eyes filled with tears. 'Please, my son, will you come with me? Will you come and see your mother and ... maybe she will forgive me.'

The young man looked at him. 'I cannot come with you. This is the only father I have ever known and I will not leave this place and these people who are my friends.'

The king begged him but his son would not leave Earthdom.

'I ask one thing,' said the king.

'You are the king,' said the young man.

'That I may bring your mother the queen to meet you here.'

'I would love to meet my mother,' said the young hunchback.

Next day the old hunchback led the king through and out of the beautiful hidden, secret valley, back to the old oak tree, and from there the king made his own way home to the palace, but said nothing to anyone.

From that time, mysteriously, the king and queen were gone from the palace for weeks at a time. No one knew where they had gone, but they were happy in the beautiful, hidden, secret valley of Earthdom.

Acknowledgements

For assistance in gathering this collection of stories I have told over the years, I would like to thank the following people: the sparkling Tom and Rhonda Muir; the adept and artistic Astrid Jaekel for the cover design; Beverley Casebow for her unrelenting encouragement, editing and tireless typing; Jennie Renton for her expertise and invaluable experience; and all the people who have freely given their tales, the Travellers, folk met on my various worldwide journeys, the diverse storytelling community, and the bewilderingly talented and helpful Donald Smith.

www.ingramcontent.com/pod-product-compliance
Lightning Source LLC
Chambersburg PA
CBHW072047110526
44590CB00018B/3073